LEARN TO PLAY GUITAR WITH
DAVE MATTHEWS BAND

By Toby Wine

Recording Credits: Doug Boduch, Guitar

Cherry Lane Music Company
Educational Director/Project Supervisor: Susan Poliniak
Director of Publications: Mark Phillips
Publications Coordinator: Rebecca Skidmore

ISBN: 978-1-60378-031-5

Visit our website at www.cherrylaneprint.com

CONTENTS

INTRODUCTION

Getting started on a new instrument is an arduous process, often made more grueling through the sheer tedium of endless repetitions of children's songs and other less-than-thrilling material. *Learn to Play Guitar with Dave Matthews Band* skirts around this potential deal-breaker by giving you a comprehensive instrumental method using examples from the music of one of today's hottest, most eclectic and exciting bands. No more "Mary Had a Little Lamb" for you—let's learn the same lessons playing "What Would You Say," "Where Are You Going," "Too Much," and more. So, let's dig in and get this thing started.

Note: Track 1 contains tuning pitches.

ABOUT THE AUTHOR

Toby Wine is a native New Yorker and a freelance guitarist, composer, arranger, and educator. He is a graduate of the Manhattan School of Music, where he studied composition with Manny Albam and Edward Green. Toby has performed with Philip Harper (of the Harper Brothers and Art Blakey's Jazz Messengers), Bob Mover, Ari Ambrose, Joe Shepley, Michael and Carolyn Leonhart (both of Steely Dan), Peter Hartmann, Ian Hendrickson Smith, and the New York–based R&B/salsa collective Melee, among others. His arrangements and compositions can be heard on recordings by Phillip Harper (*Soulful Sin, The Thirteenth Moon,* Muse Records), Ari Ambrose (*Early Song,* Steeplechase), and Ian Hendrickson Smith (*Up In Smoke,* Sharp Nine). Toby leads his own trio and septet, does studio sessions, and works as a sideman with a variety of tri-state area bandleaders. He spent four years as the music librarian for the Carnegie Hall Jazz Band and has performed orchestration and score preparation duties for jazz legend Ornette Coleman. He is the author of numerous Cherry Lane publications, including *1001 Blues Licks, The Art of Texas Blues, 150 Cool Jazz Licks in Tab, Steely Dan Legendary Licks,* and *Dave Matthews Band Under the Microscope.*

ACKNOWLEDGMENTS

Many thanks are due to Cherry Lane's head honcho, John Stix, and to my friend and editor, Susan Poliniak, for her insight, guidance, and absurdly patient good nature. Additional thanks to the extended Cherry Lane family for all that they do so well. Thanks as well to my parents, Rosemary and Jerry, and to Lissette, Bibi, Bob, Jack, Noah, Enid, Mover, Humph (R.I.P.), fellow author Karl Kaminski, and all the great teachers I've ever had.

CHAPTER 1

The Basics

Parts of the Guitar

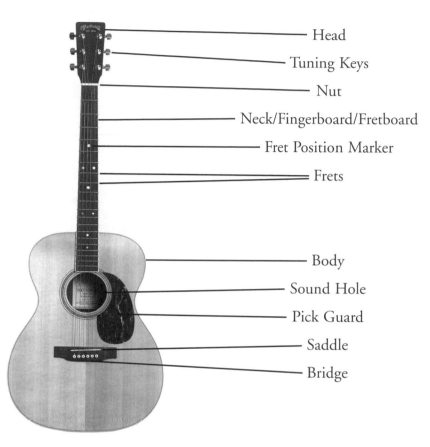

— Head
— Tuning Keys
— Nut
— Neck/Fingerboard/Fretboard
— Fret Position Marker
— Frets

— Body
— Sound Hole
— Pick Guard
— Saddle
— Bridge

How to Hold the Guitar

Good posture and correct hand positioning will go a long way toward ensuring clean, efficient technique, physical comfort, and solid tone production. Whether you're playing an acoustic or an electric, the curve in the body's lower bout should sit comfortably on your right thigh when playing in a seated position. We'll make the assumption that you're a right-hander. Southpaws, you'll need to flip-flop the right- and left-hand designations throughout this book.

Players will sometimes rest the lower bout on the left leg, with the bottom of the instrument between the legs, and employ a small footstool under the left foot to tilt the guitar into a comfortable position. This approach is usually favored by classical guitarists.

Sitting

The use of a strap can be very helpful, in that you won't need to worry about holding the guitar and can instead concentrate on getting into a comfortable playing position. Even though many rock guitarists set up the strap so that the guitar hangs very low and the arms are fully extended, this is more for aesthetics and less for technique. Having to reach down so far to get to the strings will put you in a less-than-favorable playing position and make it much harder to get the crucial arch in the your frethand fingers that's needed to play many chords and single-note phrases. Try strapping up fairly high (as Dave Matthews does) and worry about the look at a later date.

Standing

Basic Right-Hand Technique

Let's talk about the function and positioning of the hands. The right hand should be used to hold the pick between the thumb and forefinger; the pick is generally pointed in toward the body and parallel with the strings. "Choke up" on the pick so that not much more than the tip is showing between the fingers (thus lessening the chance that you'll drop it), and use small, efficient, and gentle motions. There's an inverse relationship between the strength of your pick attack and the quality of tone produced; pick too hard and your sound will all but disappear.

Holding a pick

Alternate picking, in which a *downstroke* (pick toward the floor) is alternated with an *upstroke* (toward the ceiling), is the "default mode" for this hand, and should be adhered to fairly strictly except where indicated otherwise in the music or in other obvious situations (ditto for *alternate strumming*). Chugging, low-end, heavy metal chords are often played with all downstrokes, while the off-the-beat, percussive chords employed in reggae music call for an all-upstrokes approach. When picking single notes (as opposed to strumming chords), many guitarists like to anchor the picking hand to the guitar's body in some way, often by resting the side of the hand gently on the bridge or on unused strings. It's not a necessity, but it can lend a sense of stability to the picking hand that may otherwise be lacking if it's "floating" above the strings.

If you've never tried alternate picking before, take a minute to play each of the six *open* (unfretted) strings, from the low E (6th string, the one closest to the ceiling) to the high E (1st string), playing each four times, then three times, then twice, and then once, moving from low to high and then reversing course. When you're comfortable with this, try making up some string-skipping exercises that avoid picking consecutive strings. You won't always be able to look down at your right hand as it does its work, so get used to hitting the string you want, when you want, without sounding unwanted notes on other strings.

Basic Left-Hand Technique

Your left (fretting) hand is used to change the pitches on the strings. General positioning should be in a "four fingers, four frets" alignment, meaning that if your first (index) finger plays all of the pitches on the 1st fret, your second (middle) finger plays all of the pitches on the 2nd fret, your third (ring) finger plays all of the pitches on the 3rd fret, and your pinky plays all of the pitches on the 4th fret. Use the ball of your fingertip to press down firmly into the string on the wood, between the metal frets, behind the fret that corresponds to the note you are trying to play. Many teachers suggest playing slightly closer to the higher fret for a clearer tone, but don't agonize over this too much in the beginning. As long as you avoid any actual contact with the metal frets and press the strings down with enough force, your sound should be more than adequate. Your thumb should serve as an anchor against the back of the neck, while your fretting fingers should be curved over nicely so that you won't block other strings from ringing. Playing with flat fingers (except in the case of barre chords, and we'll cover those later) is a no-no, as is any hyperextension (bending backwards) of the knuckles.

Left hand correct positioning (front)

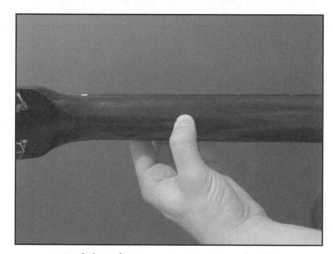

Left hand correct positioning (back)

How to Tune the Guitar

Getting your guitar in tune is actually a fairly difficult task at first and one that needs to be performed on a daily basis, at least. Guitars are extremely sensitive to changes in temperature and humidity, both of which can wreak havoc on your intonation. Try taking your guitar to the park on a hot, humid summer day, and then bringing it back inside to an air-conditioned room and you'll see what I mean.

The six strings should be tuned to the following pitches, from low (pitch) to high.

6th string:	Low E
5th string:	A
4th string:	D
3rd string:	G
2nd string:	B
1st string:	High E

Don't be confused by the seemingly paradoxical terminology used to refer to the strings; the low E string is closer to the ceiling, while the high E string is closer to the floor. The designations are based on pitch and not physical location. Note that as you move across the fretboard and toward the right side of your body, you are ascending in pitch, while moving toward the headstock will find you descending in pitch.

There are a few different methods for getting in tune. The simplest is to purchase an electric tuner that you can plug into if you play electric, or that has a little microphone to play into if you have an acoustic. With one of these tuners, the process usually involves turning the tuning key of each individual string while you play it, working toward lighting a green LED light or having a needle on a small display screen indicate that the string is in tune (the tuner should come with instructions and/or be fairly self-explanatory). Pitch pipes and tuning forks work nicely as well, but will test your ear more because you'll have to listen closely to the pitches they create and then tune a string to match the tone you're hearing.

The traditional method of tuning is the most challenging but is a must-learn for every guitarist. Ideally, you'll want to first tune your low E string to a reliable source, such as a pitch pipe, piano, keyboard, or tuning fork. Once the 6th string is in tune, play the note at its 5th fret, and then match the pitch of the next string (A) to it. Once the A string is in tune, repeat the process by playing that string's 5th-fret note (D), and then match the pitch of the 4th string (D) to it. Repeat the process for the remaining strings, but take note of one important exception: the 2nd string (B) is tuned to the 3rd string's 4th fret, not its 5th. The diagram below should make the process easy.

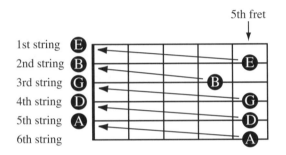

Be careful not to pull down on the fretted strings (with the fingers that are doing the fretting, that is) while tuning—this is a common tendency for beginners—as this will make the pitch you're tuning to unreliable. Also, allow the fretted pitch to ring out for at least a full second and listen to it closely before striking the untuned, open string. It will be much easier to compare the two pitches if the second doesn't come a split second after the first, which can blur any sense of distinction between the two. You may notice a subtle pulse or "beat" when you play two consecutive strings simultaneously during the tuning process. The further apart the pitches are, the quicker the beats will come. As you adjust your tuning, bringing the fretted note and open string closer to unison, the beats should slow down, ceasing entirely when you're in tune. Don't let this tuning process intimidate you. An electronic tuner is an extremely useful tool, and one that can help you get yourself properly intonated quickly, but the traditional method is essential and will help train your ears as a bonus. You won't always have a tuner handy, so get used to tuning the guitar to itself as early as possible.

How to Read Chord Diagrams

A *chord* is the sounding of two, three, four, or more pitches at the same time, or in quick succession, so that their collective ringing creates *harmony*. A barbershop quartet creates chords with their vocal harmonizing, a pianist striking multiple keys is playing chords, and a guitarist playing on two or more strings simultaneously is engaged in chord playing as well. In fact, you can break down everything a guitarist does into two general categories: chord playing and single-note playing. As you work your way through this book and get into examples taken from Matthews and the band, a wide variety of notational methods will be employed. *Standard notation* (what's usually meant by "reading music"), tablature, chord symbols, and chord diagrams will all come into play, and we'll take a moment to learn how to read each.

Chord diagrams are basically little pictures of the guitar neck shown from the perspective of a guitar on a stand in front of you. The six vertical lines represent the six strings. The horizontal lines represent the frets, beginning at the nut in the case of the thickened upper line (see the C chord below), or at another location on the neck as indicated by fret numbers to the right of the diagram (as in the D chord below). The index finger is the 1st finger ("1" in the diagrams), the middle finger is the 2nd finger ("2"), the ring finger is the 3rd ("3"), and the pinky is the 4th ("4"). The thumb gets no numeric designation as, with rare exceptions, it stays behind the neck at all times (in those rare exceptions, you may see it referred to as "T"). On top of the diagram, an "X" indicates an unplayed string, while an "O" denotes an open string that is included in the chord. The numbers below the diagram indicate the left-hand finger to be used on each string. Using the same finger on multiple strings almost always (99.9% of the time) indicates a *barre*, with the designated finger flattened across the specified strings. When barring, be sure to keep your finger as parallel with the fret metal as possible, and avoid any bending of the knuckles: The digit must be flat, straight, and true.

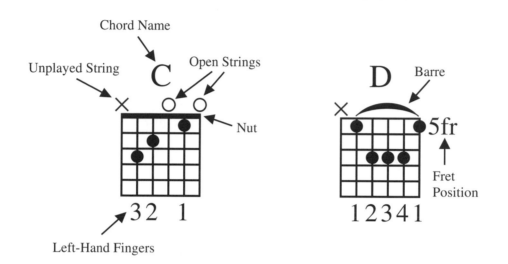

How to Read Tablature

Tablature is a notational system for guitar (and bass) that is used directly below the standard notation for the examples in this book. It features six horizontal lines representing the six strings of the guitar, the highest line being the high E (1st) string, and the lowest being the low E (6th) string. The numbers on the lines represent the frets you should play to sound the correct notes. A zero ("0") tells you to play the open string corresponding to the line on which it is shown. Multiple numbers lined up with each other indicate a chord and should be played simultaneously. In the diagram below, for instance, you would first play the notes at the 5th fret of the low E string, and then the 2nd fret of the D, G, and B strings (together).

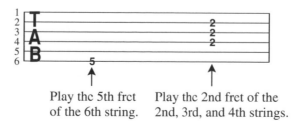

The main shortcoming of tablature is its omission of rhythmic values for the indicated notes. Without reading standard notation, or listening to a recording, it is nearly impossible to know for sure *when* and *for how long* each note should be played, although every effort has been made to place the numerals in proper relative position within each measure. On the other hand, the great thing about tab is its precision in locating the notes on the neck—in other words, *where* they should be played. For example, play the note on the low E string's 15th fret, then the A string's 10th fret, then the D string's 5th fret, and finally, the open G string. They're all the same note (G)! It's the bane of sight-reading on this stringed instrument—the fact that you can find the same exact pitch on multiple places on the neck—and tab solves the problem by telling you which of those Gs, for instance, you should play. It's no small consideration, either, because as the music gets more and more complex, positioning on the neck becomes crucial, and the wrong choice may paint you into a corner!

How to Read Standard Notation

Please put aside any fears or apprehension you may have about reading music. It's not easy, but it's not particularly hard either. Basically, it's like learning to read a new language, but it's a language with a really small vocabulary and only a few letters. Forget the complaints of friends you know who have tried to learn and quit or bellyached about it enough to discourage you from trying. A little consistency goes a long way. Once you have the principles under your belt, try a little reading every day (ten minutes or so will work just fine) and, before you know it, you'll be reading like a pro. It's an essential musical skill, and it's absolutely necessary in order to fully understand and play the music of Dave Matthews Band. Even if you can decipher the tab quickly enough, the rhythmic aspects are often the most important in their music and, as you may recall, they're not found in the tablature.

Standard notation is written on a *staff*, a grid featuring five horizontal lines, rather than the six found in tab. On the farthest left margin of the staff is a symbol called the *clef*, which indicates which notes each line and space of the staff represent. Guitarists read nearly exclusively in *treble clef*, which is also called the *G clef*.

The notes in music are represented by letter names, and there are only seven of them: A, B, C, D, E, F, and G, in ascending order. If you're playing a G and continue to rise, you go back to the beginning of the alphabet and start again at A. In other words, the 1st fret of the low E string is an F, the 3rd fret is a G, the 5th fret is an A, and the 7th fret is a B. When reading in treble clef, the spaces between the lines on the staff represent the notes F, A, C, E ("FACE") from low to high. The lines represent the notes E, G, B, D, and F, low to high ("Every Good Boy Does Fine").

Music is written and read from left to right. Barlines divide the music into organizational units called *measures* (which are also called *bars*). The *double barline* is used to indicate the end of a song or a particular section of that song.

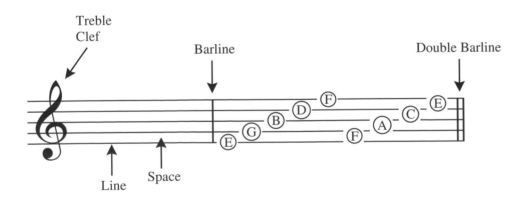

Ledger lines are used to expand the staff when the notes rise too high or sink too low to fit on the staff.

The diagram below shows the notes of the six open strings of the guitar.

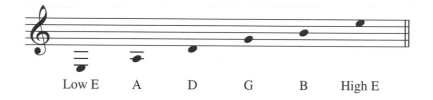

Low E   A   D   G   B   High E

The next diagram shows all of the letter-named notes using open strings, and the first three frets in both standard notation and tab.

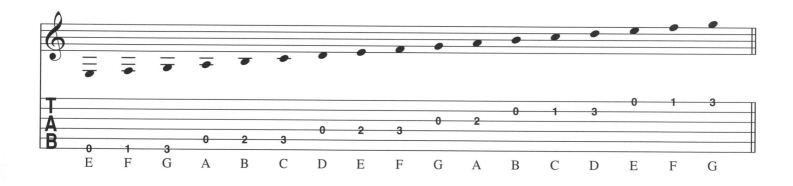

Playing through these notes is equivalent to running your hand over the white keys of a piano keyboard. But what about the black keys? These notes are called *accidentals*, and are written and referred to as either *sharps* (♯), which raise a lettered note by a *half step* (on a guitar, it's one fret) or *flats* (♭), which lower a note by a half step. Strictly speaking, there is no E♯ or B♯, and no C♭ or F♭; these are the places on the piano keyboard in which no black key is found between neighboring white keys.

C   C♯   D   D   D♭   C

Notice above, by the way, that C♯ and D♭ are the same note!

A *chromatic scale* includes all of the pitches that "fall between" the lettered notes. In the diagram below, sharps are used in an ascending chromatic scale along the lowest two strings; flats are used to descend backwards to the open low E string. Notice, again, that there's more than one way to spell a certain pitch. For example, F♯ and G♭ are the same; when this happens, you can describe F♯ as the *enharmonic equivalent* of G♭.

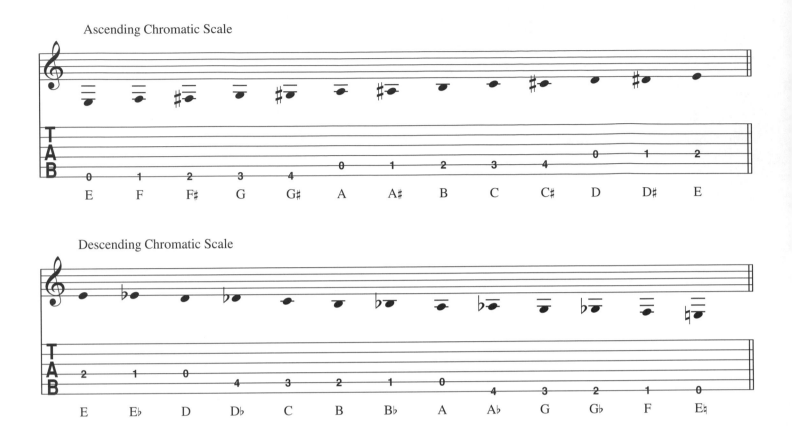

That last note in the descending scale is preceded by a *natural* symbol (♮), which returns a flat or sharp note to its non-flat/non-sharp state.

An accidental applies for the remainder of the measure in which it occurs, unless it's "cancelled out" by the use of a natural sign. In subsequent measures, the note returns automatically to its unaltered state. Often, you'll see a *courtesy accidental* in front of the first occurrence of a previously altered note to remind us of this fact.

Key Signatures

Still with me? Good. Don't worry too much if your head is spinning a bit at this point. Take your time to digest these concepts and you'll find them becoming clearer as we work our way through this book.

Yet another important concept is the *key signature*, a group of sharps or flats found immediately to the right of the clef at the beginning of a piece of music. This little group of accidentals tells us what key we're in and what notes in that key should be raised (sharped) or lowered (flatted).

For instance, three sharps—one each on the F line and the C and G spaces—indicate the key of A major. Well get into why it's called "A major" a little later on in the book, but for now you just need to know that this indicates that every F, C, and G encountered in the music should be sharped (raised a half step), unless they're temporarily changed along the way by a natural sign.

A Crash Course in Rhythm

Before you can really dive into the music of Dave Matthews Band, you'll need a bit of a crash course in reading and "feeling" a variety of rhythms. The three basic "macro" elements of music are *rhythm*, *melody*, and *harmony*. Harmony, as mentioned above, is the simultaneous or near-simultaneous sounding of pitches to create chords or "implied" chords. Melody refers to a "line" of individual pitches heard above the harmony; in pop or rock, this is often the vocal, guitar solo line, or other "singable" ideas. Rhythm, however, is *the* organizing force in music and functions much like time on a clock. Rhythm is the driving force behind the music of Dave Matthews Band, and as such will require extra scrutiny before you can really get going.

As we've already touched upon briefly, measures are used to divide music into small organizational units. Each measure has a predetermined number of beats. The *time signature*, a stack of two numerals found to the immediate right of the clef and key signature at the beginning of a piece of music, tells us this information and more.

Deciphering a time signature is easy. The top number tells us how many beats are in each measure, while the bottom number tells us the rhythmic value of a single beat. For instance, 4/4, the most common time signature by far, means four beats per measure, with each beat lasting for a single quarter note. The lower number may sometimes be an eight (so each beat lasts an eighth note) or, more uncommonly, a two (half note) or 16 (16th note). The chart below illustrates the various types of rhythmic values, their equivalent rests (silences), and their durations in 4/4 time.

Name	Symbol	Equivalent Rest	Duration (in 4/4)
Whole Note	𝅝	▬	Four Beats
Half Note	𝅗𝅥	▬	Two Beats
Quarter Note	𝅘𝅥	𝄽	One Beat
Eighth Note	𝅘𝅥𝅮	𝄾	Half of a Beat
Sixteenth Note	𝅘𝅥𝅯	𝄿	Quarter of a Beat
Thirty-Second Note	𝅘𝅥𝅰	𝅀	Eighth of a Beat

By examining the chart closely, you should be able to discern that there are four quarters in a measure. This can also be broken down into eight eighth notes (two per each quarter note beat), 16 16th notes (four per each quarter note), and so on. Eighth, 16th, and 32nd notes are often beamed together when occurring consecutively within a beat, as shown below:

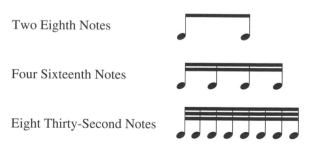

Two Eighth Notes

Four Sixteenth Notes

Eight Thirty-Second Notes

Eighth notes are often verbalized with the use of the word "and" to represent any notes that fall in between the numbered beats. In other words, a measure of eight eighth notes would be verbalized as "1–and–2–and–3–and–4–and," with each syllable given equal duration. Sixteenth notes are verbalized by breaking down each beat into four parts as "1–ee–and–a–2–ee–and–a," etc., again, with each syllable of exactly equal length. Musicians will often say things like "that lick starts on the '2–and,'" meaning the eighth note falling in between beats 2 and 3, or "come in on the 'ee' of beat 3," meaning you should enter on the second 16th note of beat 3.

Triplets divide beats or measures into three equal parts and are usually verbalized as "tri-ple-et" or "1–triplet, 2–triplet," once again with each syllable lasting for the same duration. The diagram below illustrates the various types of triplets stacked above a series of four quarter notes. Eighth note triplets divide a quarter note into three equal pieces; quarter note triplets divide a half note into three equal pieces, and so on.

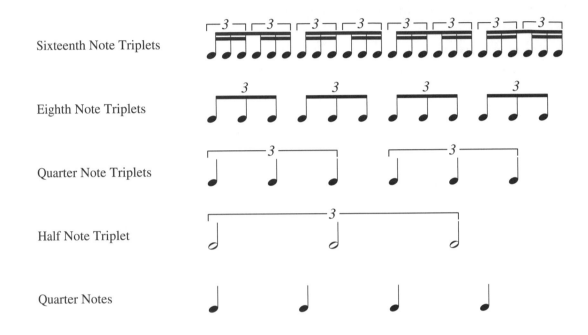

Finally, two other concepts important to reading and understanding rhythms are *dots* and *ties*. A dot immediately following a given note instructs you to increase its rhythmic duration by half; in other words, a dotted half note lasts three beats, not two, while a dotted quarter note lasts one and a half beats instead of one. So, a dot gives a note 150% of its standard ("undotted") value.

A tie connects one note to another and combines the total value; only the first note is struck and is then allowed to sustain for the combined total. In other words, a half note tied to a quarter note lasts two and a half beats, while a whole note tied to a quarter note lasts five. Ties can and often do cross over bar lines, but dots never do. Rests can be dotted, but are never tied. Don't worry too much if this is a bit confusing; we'll have plenty of opportunities to explore these ideas further as we dig into the songs to follow.

Let's do some rhythmic drills to be sure that you're digesting (at least some of) this. You can tap the following rhythms out on a tabletop or play them on a single open string of your guitar. The diamond-shaped whole and half notes and slash-topped quarters, eighths, and 16ths are often used to signify a rhythm with no specific pitch to be played. Take a shot at the first exercise, an eight-measure phrase that mixes whole, half, and quarter notes. Proceed at a slow, consistent *tempo* (pace) while tapping out a steady quarter note pulse with your foot (this should really help to orient yourself within each measure).

By the way, the dotted double bar lines at the beginning and end of the phrase are *repeats*; they signify that you should repeat the music that appears between them.

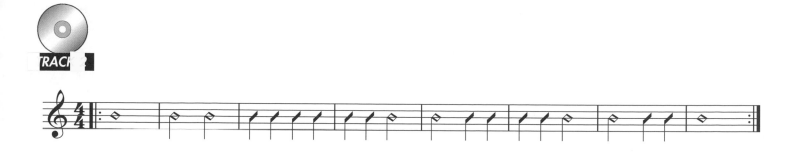

The next exercise lasts 12 measures and adds rests, dots, and ties to the mix. You may want to try counting each beat out loud or, failing that challenge (like the proverbial walking and chewing gum at the same time), counting in your head so that you know where you are in each measure. Remember to attack only the first note when a tie occurs, and then hold it out for the duration of the tied notes.

Let's make it even harder with the addition of eighth notes, eighth note rests, and dotted and tied eighth note figures as well. Count the notes that fall between the beats as "ands." In other words, the third note in both the 4th and 5th measures falls on the "2–and," while the first note in measures 9 and 10 falls on the "1–and."

It's crucial when learning anything new—and challenging music in particular—that you work through things slowly and patiently, repeating as often as necessary until your results are perfect. Let's throw 16th notes—which dominate the music of Dave Matthews Band—into the mix as we ratchet things up another notch.

Getting tougher, huh? Don't worry—you'll be given plenty of opportunities to practice your skills in the coming chapters.

This last exercise is pretty difficult, but should help to get you ready to tackle the band's music in the pages to come. The broken 16th note figures below, awash in rests and off-kilter rhythms, are encountered repeatedly in the songs of Matthews and his colleagues. Once again, don't get discouraged: Take your time and repeat things (even if they're just individual measures) as necessary. Count each beat out if you need to, using the "1–ee–and–a, 2–ee–and–a" verbalizations that break each beat into four equal pieces. Be analytical and exacting. Never rely on instinct or guess where a note falls—figure it out instead and play it with confidence and authority. Even if your progress is slower at first, you'll ultimately improve as a guitarist much more quickly.

CHAPTER 2

Single-Note Lines and Scales, Plus More on Key Signatures and Intervals

Now that we've gotten the fundamentals out of the way, let's look at some single-note lines taken from Dave Matthews Band songs and talk about how to decipher and play them.

The examples below will get progressively harder as they go along, and feature not only guitar but also vocal, horn, and keyboard parts (arranged for guitar, or course) as well. Play each example very slowly and repeat it as many times as needed until you've gotten it down cold. Patience is indeed a virtue, and for the beginning guitarist it's an absolute necessity. Independence of your fretting-hand fingers and coordination between the two hands in general takes a long time to develop. Think of a basketball player working on his free throws. Does he or she heave the ball at the basket two or three times and call it a day? Of course not. They'll put up two or three *hundred* shots during a practice session, and strive for the same fundamentally sound mechanics every time. That's not to say that you have to play each example that follows 200 times in a row, but you will need to dig deeply into your reserve of patience and perseverance if you want to build yourself a strong technical foundation on the guitar.

Single-Note Lines

Our first example is taken from the keyboard part that accompanies John Popper's harmonica solo on "What Would You Say," the band's first big hit. Because of the simple rhythms here (all whole notes) you can give the pitches your undivided attention. Play this one in *2nd position* with your index finger playing all of the 2nd-fret notes while your middle and ring fingers take the notes on the 3rd and 4th frets, respectively, and your pinky gets that 5th-fret note (by the way, whenever you see a position, the number indicates where your left-hand fingering begins—here, it's the 2nd fret). Stretch with your pinky to grab the final B on the high E string's 7th fret. Although the tab makes it easy to see where each note is located, be sure to look at the standard notation as well, as it's important to recognize notes on the staff and have the ability to translate them to the fretboard. Also, note the key signature next to the treble clef at the beginning of the example: three sharps, the key of A major. This means that all F, C, and G pitches are raised a half step (one fret), but note that in measure 7, a natural symbol lowers that G.

"What Would You Say" Keyboard Part from *Under the Table and Dreaming*

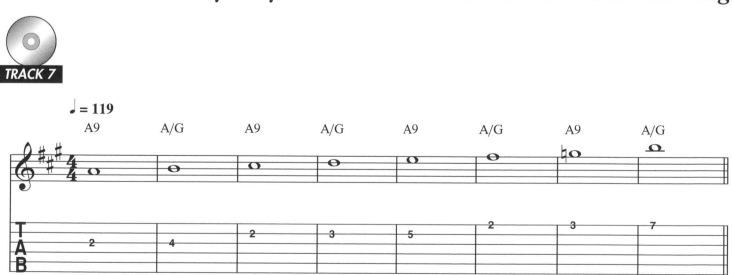

Now try Matthews' vocal line from the chorus of the same song. Play this in 1st position (also called *open position*, because it generally uses open-string notes), using your index finger for the Cs on the B string's 1st fret, and your middle finger for the A on the G string (2nd fret). The rhythm here is a bit more involved, with a rest on the 1st beat (the line begins on beat 2), and a tie on the last eighth note (on the "and" of beat 4) that holds it over into the next measure. Once again, take note of the key signature and the natural signs applied to both the C and G pitches, but note that the natural in the first measure alters all three of those Cs.

"What Would You Say" Vocal Line from *Under the Table and Dreaming*

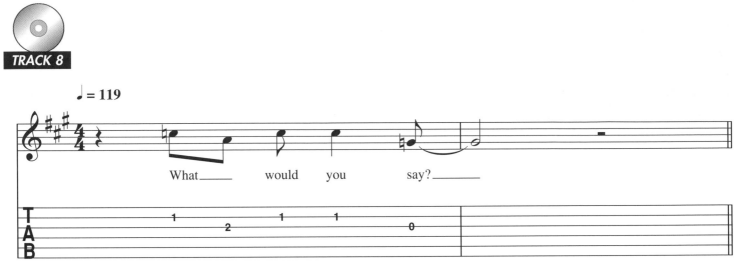

Let's continue with a few more of Dave's vocal lines. The next one is taken from "So Much" and combines a measure of steady eighth notes with a second measure including dots and ties. As with our previous example, this one should be played in 1st position, with the index and middle fingers taking the 1st and 2nd fret notes, respectively. Use strict alternate picking throughout, beginning with a downstroke, and count out the second measure carefully so that each note falls in its proper place (the second "long" is played on the "and" of beat 2 and is sustained until the word "time," which falls on beat 4).

"So Much to Say" Vocal Line from *Crash*

Next up is Dave's vocal from the same song's bridge. Play this one in 2nd position (index finger playing all 2nd-fret notes). Begin with a half note rest, so that your first note (C♯) falls on beat 3 of the opening measure. The dotted half note D in measure 2 lasts three beats, followed by a quarter note rest on beat 4. Measure 3 has you resting on beat 1, then playing quarter notes on beats 2, 3, and 4, while measure 4 includes a steady stream of eighth notes (two per beat), with the final note tied over into measure 5.

"So Much to Say" Bridge Vocal from *Crash*

Written by David J. Matthews, Peter M. Griesar, and Boyd Tinsley
© 1996 Colden Grey, Ltd. (ASCAP)
International Copyright Secured   All Rights Reserved

"Where Are You Going" was featured in the Adam Sandler movie *Mr. Deeds,* and it remains one of the band's most popular and memorable songs. The example below is based on Matthews' opening vocal melody and should be played in 2nd position, with the ring finger taking the opening note on the D string's 4th fret.

"Where Are You Going" Vocal Line from *Busted Stuff*

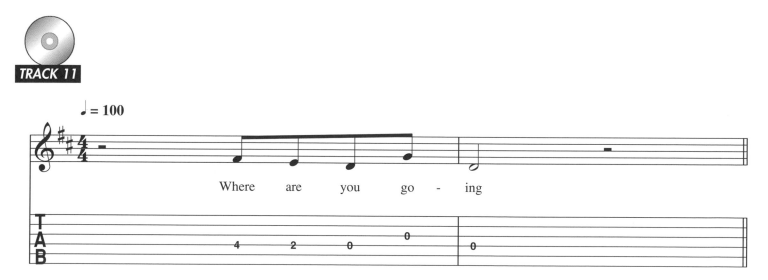

Written by David J. Matthews
© 2002 David J. Matthews (ASCAP)
International Copyright Secured   All Rights Reserved

This next example is taken from the song's chorus and begins on beat 2 after a quarter note rest. Play it in 1st position (index finger on the 1st-fret Cs) and count out the 2nd measure even if you're familiar with the song. The dotted eighth note (on "Su") means the 2nd note in the measure ("per") falls on the "a" of beat 1 (remember those 16th note verbalizations?). That note is tied over to an eighth note, meaning that "man" falls on the "and" of beat 2.

"Where Are You Going" Chorus Vocal from *Busted Stuff*

Our final vocal line is taken from "Captain" and includes a dotted eighth–16th note figure in the first measure much like the one in the previous example. Be sure to count out the final two measures, which include some slightly off-kilter rhythms. The word "this" falls on the "and" of beat 3, while "ship" falls on the "and" of beat 4 before rising a fret to begin measure 3. The final dotted quarter note also falls on the "and" of beat 3.

"Captain" Chorus Vocal from *Busted Stuff*

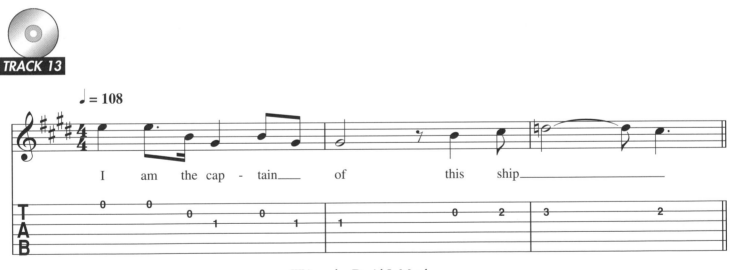

More *syncopated* ("off the beat") rhythms await in the following excerpt from "What Would You Say." Play it in 1st position, using your index finger for the 1st-fret notes and your ring finger for the 3rd-fret notes. Don't lift your finger from the high E string to the B string for these two—instead, *roll* it down without coming off the fingerboard and let both ring out together. Essentially, your finger becomes a "barre" across the strings; we'll explore this technique at length later in this book as we deal with barres that cross all six strings at once. The first note in each measure falls on the "and" of beat 1, while the second falls on the "and" of beat 3.

By the way, that "let ring" indication means that in measure 1 you should let that E ring out while you play the B, and then in measure 2 you should let that G ring out while you play the D (by using that "roll" technique with your ring finger, as described above).

"What Would You Say" Pre-Chorus Fill from *Under the Table and Dreaming*

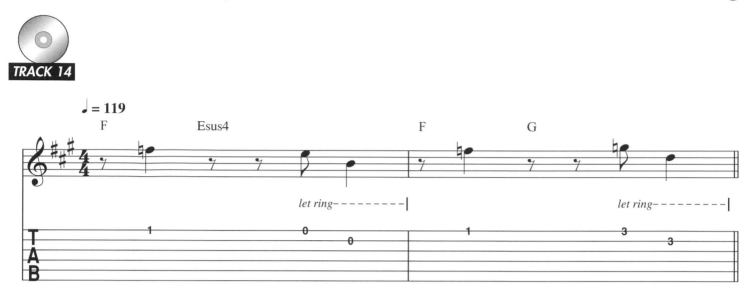

Finally, let's shift gears a bit for this open string lick from "Warehouse." The subtler of two layered guitar parts, it's a great exercise for practicing your alternate picking. You can leave your left hand off the neck entirely as you alternate strictly between down and upstrokes while keeping up a steady stream of 16th notes. It's a typical Matthews phrase in that the group of 16 pitches is broken down into an unusual pattern (3-2-3-3-1-4) as it jumps between the open B and high E strings. This goes by fairly quickly on the recording, but resist the urge to work faster than you can effectively play. Clean, precise picking is the goal here, not sloppy speed. The ability to play quickly will arrive sooner than you might think if you're consistent with your practicing and patient about your tempos.

"Warehouse" Verse Lick from *Under the Table and Dreaming*

Common Scales

Before we move onto other topics, a short discussion of scales is in order. A scale is a series of single notes from which melodies and chords can be derived. The *major scale* is the most common, and is the basis (along with its variations) for the vast majority of music in the Western world. The major scale is constructed by following a specific series of intervals. These intervals are as follows:

whole step–whole step–half step–whole step–whole step–whole step–half step.

A *whole step*, by the way, is equal to two half steps. On a guitar, an interval of a whole step would be notes that are two frets apart (e.g., C and D, on the 1st and 3rd frets of the B string).

In G major, this scale would be: G–A–B–C–D–E–F♯–G.

Here it is written out on the staff.

Notice that it's written out with the key signature of G major, which has one sharped note in it (F♯). We'll talk more about keys and key signatures in a moment.

Each of these notes can be thought of as a number. There's the 1 or 1st degree (here, G), which is also called the *root* or *tonic*, then the 2nd (A), 3rd (B), 4th (C), 5th (D), 6th (E), and 7th (F♯), and then the numbering begins all over again at the 1st (G again). The distance from any note to the next time it occurs either higher or lower is called an *octave*. So, the G on the top of the staff is one octave higher than the G on the second line from the bottom.

By following this pattern of half and whole steps, you can construct a major scale beginning on any note. The diagram below shows the E and G major scales in two-octave fingerings.

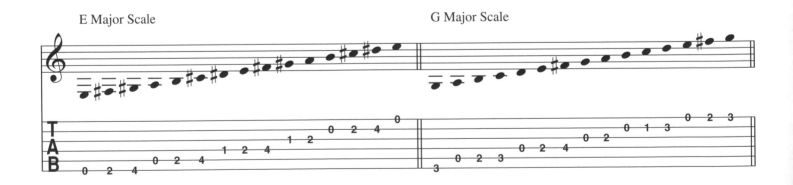

Once you've gotten those two major scales comfortably under your fingers, try this somewhat more difficult but much more common and practical fingering for the G major scale in 2nd position. Remember, your index finger will play all of the notes on the 2nd fret, your middle finger will play all of those on the 3rd, your ring finger will play the 4th-fret notes, and your pinky will take on all of the 5th-fret notes.

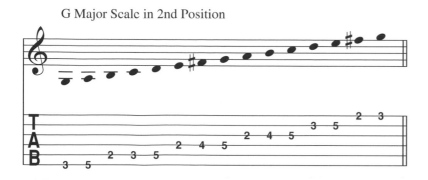

The nice thing about this fingering is that because it avoids open strings, it is a *moveable* form. So, if you need a G# major scale, you just move everything up one fret (i.e., toward the guitar's body). Go up one more fret and you've got an A major scale. Play this form in both directions (ascending and descending) and get it memorized as soon as possible—it's an absolute essential.

Another absolute must is the *minor pentatonic scale*, a five-note scale as common in rock 'n' roll as long hair and Marshall stacks. The diagram below shows the scale in E using open strings, and then in G in its more familiar moveable form. Note that, unlike the moveable major scale, the moveable minor pentatonic begins with the index finger, not the middle finger.

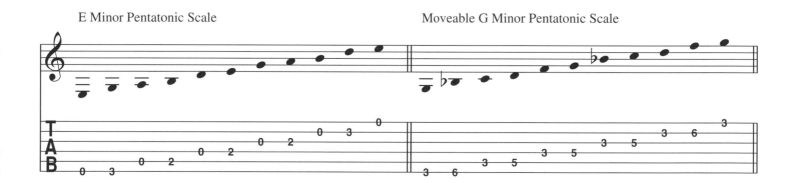

By the way, the minor pentatonic scale is based on the *minor* scale. Here's how the minor scale is spelled, interval-wise.

whole step–half step–whole step–whole step–half step–whole step–whole step.

So, the G minor scale would be: G–A–B♭–C–D–E♭–F–G. Below are a couple of common moveable fingerings.

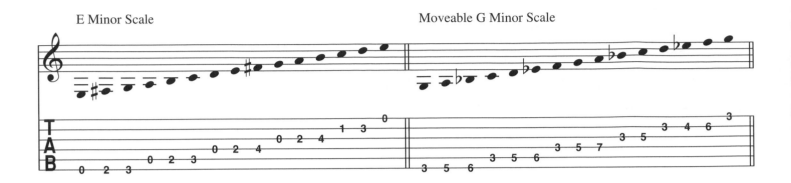

"Spider" Exercise

Lastly, the example below is the "spider" exercise, a series of single notes that's not quite a scale but should help you to develop left-hand finger independence and coordination with the pick. It's merely four consecutive notes using all four fingers on each of the six strings. Try playing it straight up and down, doubling, tripling, and quadrupling each note, or shuffling the sequence of the notes on each string. For example, instead of using your 1st, 2nd, 3rd, and 4th fingers in a row, try a 1–3–2–4 sequence or any other variation you can come up with. It may not be the most musical exercise there is, but it's one that's given many a fledgling guitarist a useful technical kickstart. The "spider" is shown below beginning on A (the 5th fret of the low E string) but can be moved around and played anywhere on the neck.

More on Key Signatures

Now that you know about major and minor scales, you can fully grasp the concepts of keys and key signatures. Keys are named according to their first note and their *quality* (e.g., major or minor).

Here is a chart of all possible major and minor keys and their key signatures. Note that a key signature can stand for a major *or* a minor key. You can tell what key a song is in by listening. Does the music return more often to one chord or note? Does it begin on a particular chord or note (this is usually a dead giveaway)? Also, major and minor sound very different from each other—major often sounds "happier" than minor.

Key Signature	Major Key	Minor Key
	C Major	A Minor
	G Major	E Minor
	D Major	B Minor
	A Major	F♯ Minor
	E Major	C♯ Minor
	B Major	G♯ Minor
	F♯ Major/G♭ Major	D♯ Minor/E♭ Minor
	D♭ Major	B♭ Minor
	A♭ Major	F Minor
	E♭ Major	C Minor
	B♭ Major	G Minor
	F Major	D Minor

A Note on Intervals

You've already learned about half steps and whole steps, so here's the rest of the primer on intervals. This sort of knowledge will prove useful when we get more into chords and how they're built.

The interval (distance) between any two notes can be described with a combination of a number and a quality. Remember how each note in the scale was assigned a number? That comes into play here.

In order to determine the interval between two notes, you first take the bottom note and count up by letters (i.e., by lettered notes, never counting the same letter twice). Say that we're trying to find the distance between C and E. Start with C as "1" and then count up to E, which is "3." What this tells you is that C and E are a 3rd apart. Easy, huh? Well, there's just a little more to it than that.

You need to know the *quality* of the interval. For this part, you just refer to the major scale that begins on the lowest note. Take a look at this chart.

1	Root
2	Major 2nd
3	Major 3rd
4	Perfect 4th
5	Perfect 5th
6	Major 6th
7	Major 7th
8	Perfect Octave

Let's say that you want to find the distance between a C and the E just above it. Take the bottom note, C, and think of its major scale. Is the note E a member of this scale? It certainly is! That means that the E is a *major 3rd* away from the C. It's that simple—you just name the interval according to the little chart above. By the way, for these "major" notes, you can refer to them by just the number—you don't need to add in "major" or "perfect" unless you want to be specific.

But what if the second note *isn't* a member of the major scale? What if that second note above is E♭? Well, then you need to add a little qualifier onto the name. Here are the rules.

- When *major* intervals are lowered by a half step, they become *minor.*
- When *perfect* and *minor* intervals are lowered by a half step, they become *diminished.*
- When *major* and *perfect* intervals are raised by a half step, they become *augmented.*

So, E♭ is a *minor 3rd* away from C.

You don't need to go crazy with memorizing this at this stage—it's just something you may wish to refer back to as you work along.

CHAPTER 3

Power Chords

Power chords are compact, two-note units used frequently in all styles of rock, and occasionally in other genres as well. They're fairly easy to play, can be moved all over the neck quickly, and sound great when played through a cranked-up amplifier. The power chord combines the root (the lowest note in the chord, and the note which gives the chord it its name), and a second note on the next consecutive higher string that is a 5th above the root; sometimes, the root is doubled at the octave as well (i.e., the note one octave higher than the root is played, too).

Power chords are played primarily on the lower-pitched strings and should be played with the index finger on the root and the ring finger playing the higher note(s). Try the exercise below, which begins with a sustained, two-note power chord (represented by the chord symbol G5), and then slides the shape up and down the low E and A strings a fret at a time. Don't lift your fingers off the neck as you shift up and down: Simply release pressure and slide to the next targeted chord. You shouldn't hear a gap between each chord, but you shouldn't hear a lot of sliding string noise either.

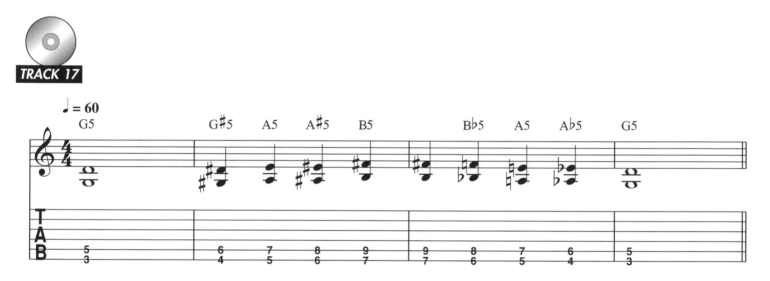

Now let's try an exercise that adds a third note to each power chord. Flatten your ring finger into a barre to play both of the higher notes on the A and D strings. Try to keep the ring-finger barre fairly parallel to the fret wire and, as much as possible, avoid bending your knuckles. The phrase below descends from an A5 chord all the way down to an E5 shape that incorporates the open low E string.

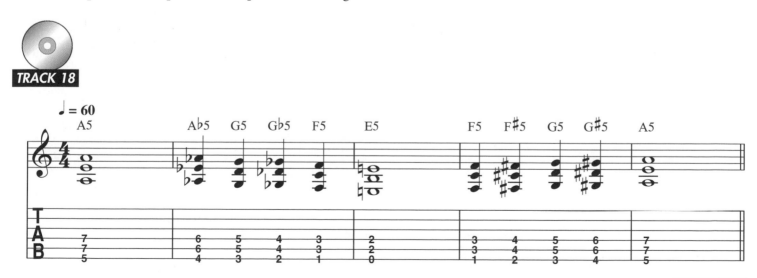

Next, let's try a few examples from Dave Matthews Band songs. The first is a tiny segment from "Crush" that features a repeated C5 chord in an eighth note rhythm.

"Crush" Excerpt from *Before These Crowded Streets*

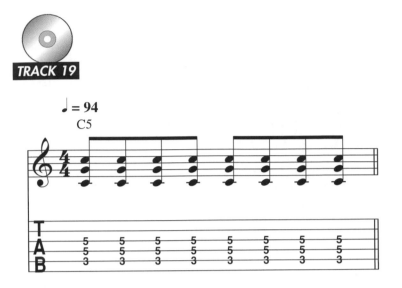

It's a piece of cake, right? How about this one from "Louisiana Bayou"? It follows up descending three-note power chords moving two frets at a time with single notes that follow the same rhythm. Play the single-note lines in 2nd position, with your middle finger taking the 3rd-fret notes and your ring finger taking the 4th-fret C♯s on the A string. In each measure, the first note falls on beat 2, the next note falls on the "a" of beat 2, and the last note falls on the "and" of 3.

"Louisiana Bayou" Bridge Riff from *Stand Up*

This next example includes one of the two layered guitar parts setting up the groove immediately preceding Matthew's vocal entrance on the funk hit "Too Much." The "x" marks that are used in place of regular noteheads (and appear in the tab as well) indicate a muffled sound created by releasing left-hand pressure without lifting your fingers from the strings. In other words, every time you see an "x" in the example, stay in the F♯5 shape but don't press down; you should only hear a muted, percussive attack instead of any specific pitches. Play the E7sus4 chord by lifting off the strings entirely and striking the open low E, A, and D strings. Keep your fingers close by, as you'll have to follow up quickly with a couple of F♯5 chords.

"Too Much" Verse Riff from *Crash*

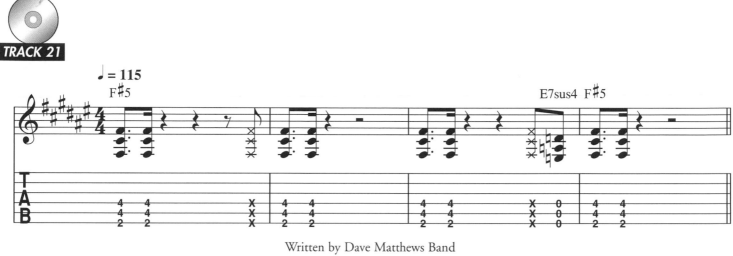

Written by Dave Matthews Band
© 1996 Carter Beauford, Boyd Tinsley, Stefan Lessard, LeRoi Moore, and David J. Matthews (ASCAP)
International Copyright Secured   All Rights Reserved

Try these final two measures from "The Dreaming Tree" interlude, which descend from A5 to F5 and E5 and incorporate more muted tones along the way. The time signature here is 6/8, which means that there are six beats in each measure and each eighth note lasts for one beat. There are three other new notational symbols to be aware of here. The widening angle beneath the F5 chords indicates a *crescendo*, a gradual increase in volume achieved by picking just a little bit harder each time. The smaller, reversed shape beneath the E5 chord that looks like a "v" turned on its side is an *accent* mark, which tells you to give the final chord an added emphasis by hitting it fairly hard with the pick. The dotted half circle above the chord is a *fermata*, which indicates that the chord is to be sustained indefinitely.

"The Dreaming Tree" Interlude Ending from *Before These Crowded Streets*

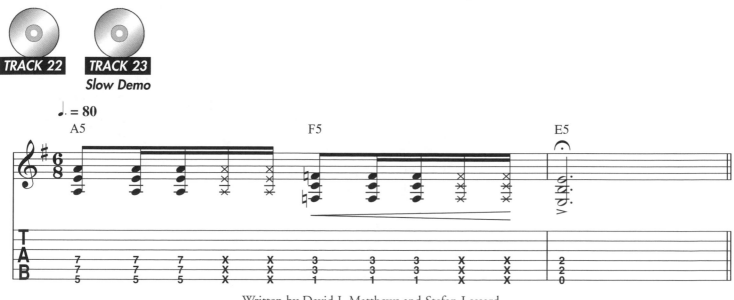

Written by David J. Matthews and Stefan Lessard
© 1998 David J. Matthews and Stefan Lessard (ASCAP)
International Copyright Secured   All Rights Reserved

Finally, let's look at a longer excerpt from "Crush" which serves as the accompaniment to Boyd Tinsley's violin solo. This one is played with a *swing feel*, meaning that the 16th notes in the example are not played precisely evenly. Instead, each group of two 16th notes is to be played as if they were the 1st and 3rd notes of a 16th note triplet. It's an advanced concept that's most easily understood by simply listening to the song or excerpt rather than by spending a lot of time intellectualizing it. Here's the bottom line: Give it a listen and note the difference between this and a *straight feel* in which beats are divided evenly (it's what you've been playing so far in this book).

Some other technical considerations apply to this example as well. The muted tones should be approached with the technique discussed earlier, except in the case of the E chords (play these with the middle, ring, and index fingers on the A, D, and G strings, respectively). Because of the open low E string, you'll have to create the muted sound by using the side of your picking hand to muffle the strings by resting it gently across them close to the guitar's bridge. There are also two slides in the phrase that should be played by striking the G on the low E string's 15th fret with your index finger, and then sliding down the neck toward the 7th or 8th fret. Keep the pressure on the string as you move down quickly—you shouldn't hear distinct, individual tones as you slide, but the note should sound as if it's falling off sharply.

"Crush" Violin Solo Riff from *Before These Crowded Streets*

TRACK 24

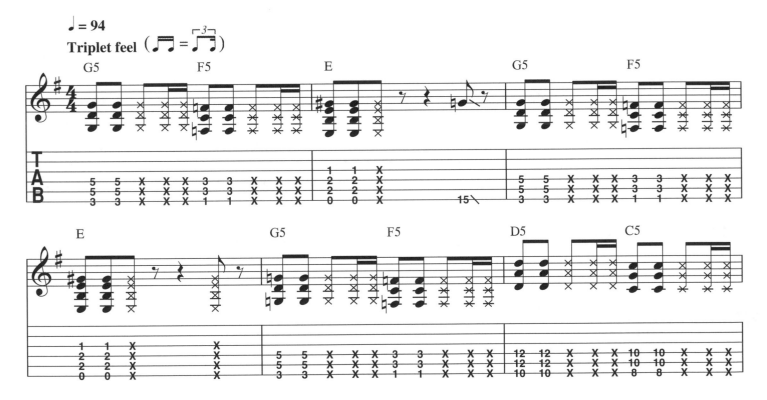

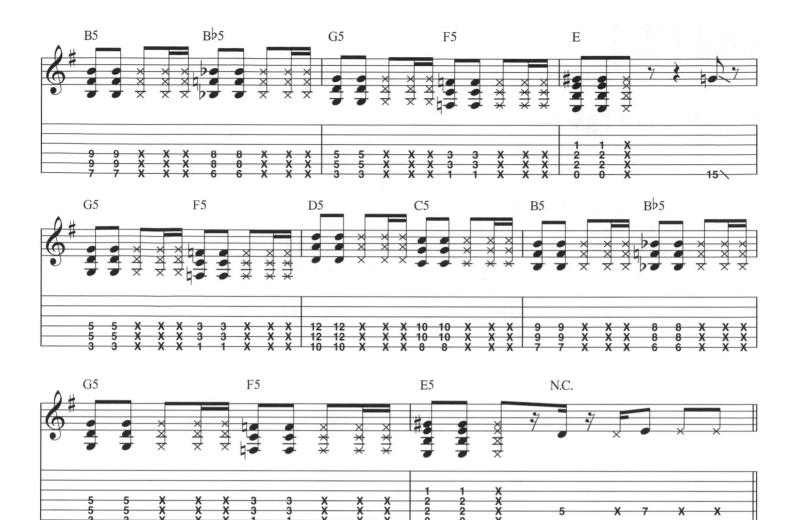

CHAPTER 4

Open-Position Chords

Open-position chords—those that include at least one and often multiple open strings—are often some of the first things a beginning guitarist is taught. The chord diagrams below illustrate the most common open-position chord shapes, some of which should be familiar to you if you've been playing for even a short while. Although these most common forms don't appear all too frequently in Dave Matthews Band's songs, they *are* used occasionally and, in combination with the scales examined earlier, can serve as the foundation of solid technique upon which your playing can eventually grow into something formidable. In simpler terms, if you can't switch smoothly between G major and C major chords or play a G major scale, you won't be tearing up the stage à la Jimi Hendrix anytime soon. Take your time getting these chords under your fingers and work on combining them into progressions, putting a particular emphasis on the chords that are the hardest for you to play.

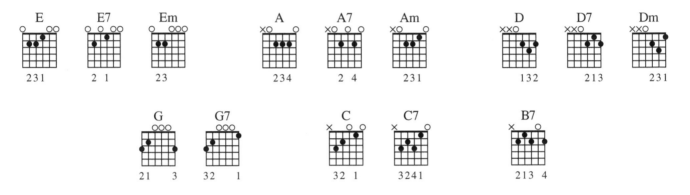

Now let's take a look at a few examples from Dave Matthews Band songs. The first is taken from the final two measures of "Captain" and simply moves from C to G major. Note the muted open A string in the latter chord, which can be achieved by simply flattening your middle finger (playing the root on the low E string) ever so slightly to muffle the open string.

"Captain" Ending Chords from *Busted Stuff*

TRACK 25

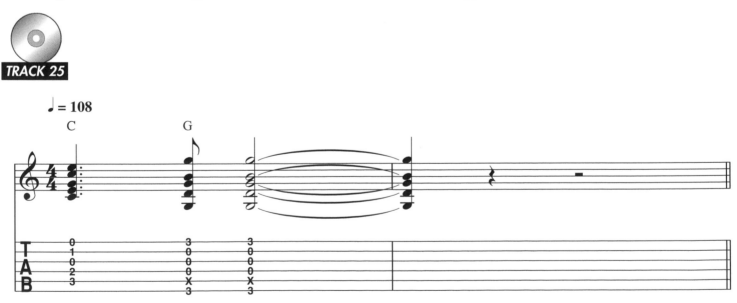

Written by David J. Matthews
© 2002 David J. Matthews (ASCAP)
International Copyright Secured   All Rights Reserved

This next excerpt is taken from the bridge of the same song and mixes open-position A and E chords with a B5 power chord shape and some single-note lines. The E chord is first played on the lowest four strings alone, with the open B and high E strings added quickly after, but it is played in its complete, six-string voicing on beat 4 of measure 1. In measure 2, play both the B5 chord and Bb5 single notes with your index finger on the A string and your ring finger barring the D and G strings. Release left-hand pressure without lifting off the strings to create the muted tones, each indicated by an "x" in the notation.

"Captain" Bridge Riff from *Busted Stuff*

We'll end our discussion of open-position chords with the following example from the bridge of "Drive In Drive Out." The first thing to be aware of here is the 6/8 time signature—remember that this means that there are six beats in every measure and an eighth note lasts a single beat. A quick glance at the example's first measure reveals a quarter note, two eighth notes tied to each other, and another quarter note. Each of these chords is equal in duration (dividing the measure into three equal parts) and should last for two eighth note beats. The movement from A to D to C is pretty much meat-and-potatoes Guitar 101, so if these transitions give you trouble, slow them down and repeat them until they're second nature. There's a glimpse of Matthew's unique chord approach (more on that later) in the unusual Dadd4 voicing at the end of measure 3, which is played by simply shifting each of your fingers up two frets from their positions in the C major chord preceding it. The phrase ends with a two-measure riff on the D and open A strings that many will recognize as a familiar beginner's blues pattern.

"Drive In Drive Out" Bridge Chords from *Crash*

Written by David J. Matthews
© 1996 David J. Matthews (ASCAP)
International Copyright Secured   All Rights Reserved

But before we leave this chapter, here's a quick note of explanation on that Dadd4 chord. All that the "add4" means is that you should—ready?—add to the chord the note a 4th above the root. Here, it means to add a G (you can get to it by considering D as 1, and then counting up—the fourth note is G). Often, you'll omit the 5th when you "add 4" to a chord (notice that, here, the A—the 5th—is indeed missing).

CHAPTER 5

More Chord Basics and Barre Chords

A Little Chord Primer

You've already been playing chords for a while now, but it's good to know how they're constructed. *Triads* are three-note chords; they consist of a root, plus a 3rd (counted up from the root of the chord), plus a 5th (also counted up from the root). Here's a chart that shows how triads are built from a scale (here, C major), but you can think of this as skipping every other note and then stacking things up.

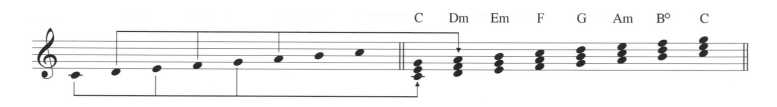

Triads built on major and minor scales can be major, minor, or diminished. That B chord with the funny symbol after it is a *diminished* chord. *Major* chords contain a root, plus one note a major 3rd higher and another a minor 3rd above that. *Minor* chords contain a root, plus one note a minor 3rd higher and another a major 3rd above that; minor chords are indicated by an "m" in the name (e.g., Dm, Em, and Am, above). *Diminished* chords contain a root, plus one note a minor 3rd higher and another a minor 3rd above that; they're indicated by a little circle in the name, or the letters "dim."

Four-note chords built in a similar fashion to triads (the "every other note" method) are called *7th chords;* you can recognize them by a "7" in a chord's name. By the way, 7th chords built on the 5th degree of the scale are given the name *dominant 7th* chords, and chords built on the 7th degree are *minor 7th ♭5th chords* (also referred to as *half diminished*).

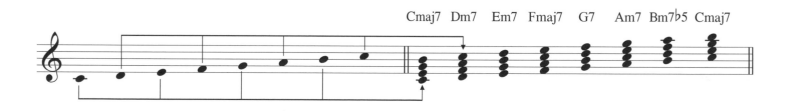

As long as we remain *diatonic*—that is, within one key and without using *borrowed tones* (i.e., notes that are not members of that particular key)—the qualities of these chords remain constant and can be referred to by Roman numerals representing the steps of the major scale. In a major key, I is always major, iii is always minor (note that lower-case letters are used for minor and diminished chords), IV is major, etc. Progressions can be described with these numerals and can be transposed easily to other keys using this approach. For example, I–IV–V in C would be C–F–G, in E it would be E–A–B, etc.

Now, on to barre chords . . .

Barre Chords

Barre chords require you to flatten a single finger across several strings on the same fret. The other fingers are often added to grab notes on higher (or, less commonly, lower) frets. We've already seen an example of these barres in action during our discussion of three-note power chords in which the root is played by the index finger while the ring finger barres the two upper notes together. The diagram below illustrates the six most common barre chord shapes, three each with roots on the low E and A strings covering major, minor, and dominant 7th chord varieties.

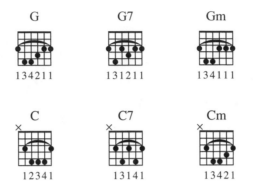

Note that the index finger provides the barre in all of these cases, spanning all six strings in the case of chords with roots on the low E string, and five in those with roots on the A string. Barre chords are a definite step up on the difficulty scale from open-position chords, but they're just as essential. They'll eventually become second nature to you through persistent, patient practicing. Try barring just a few of the higher strings at a time at first, using only the index finger, and then gradually add in each of the remaining lower strings. Don't worry about adding any other fingers until you can cleanly barre all six strings. You can check the integrity of your barre by picking each string individually to confirm that it's ringing clearly. After you've developed some facility with the single-finger barre technique, invent your own progressions combining barre chords with roots on both the low E and A strings, including each of the varieties illustrated above. One of the big keys to getting these chords to sound right is to keep your index finger as close to parallel with the fret wire as possible; avoid any bending of the knuckles. If the finger's not straight and true, you won't be able to hear all of the notes in the chord.

Once you're ready, take a crack at the following excerpts from the band, beginning with this short phrase from "Warehouse."

"Warehouse" Chorus Riff from *Under the Table and Dreaming*

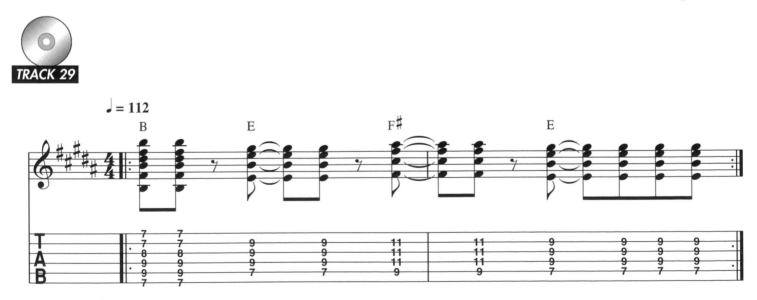

Written by David J. Matthews
© 1994 David J. Matthews (ASCAP)
International Copyright Secured   All Rights Reserved

The example below, from "So Much to Say," shifts a single, major-chord barre shape up and down in parallel fashion, illustrating the convenience of these chord forms. If you're on an A major chord and need an A♭ major, simply move the shape down one fret (try doing that with an open position chord—you can't). As you play the riff below, release pressure by lifting up slightly, without removing your fingers from the strings, each time you encounter an "x" in the notation. Use the same technique as you move the chord up and down, keeping your hand in the barre chord shape and avoiding the need to "reset" your fingers at each new fret location. The strumming pattern here employs one of Matthews' favorite rhythmic techniques—dividing a group of 16th notes into smaller, uneven groupings by way of accents and muted chords.

"So Much to Say" Bridge Riff from *Crash*

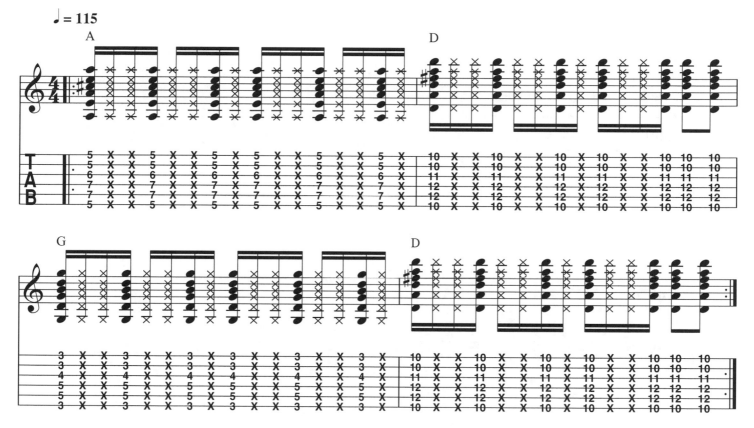

The vigorously strummed barre-chord part below, from "What Would You Say," includes both major and minor shapes along the low E string, as well as a new chord in measure 5, Esus4 (by the way, a "sus4" chord is essentially a chord with a 4th instead of a 3rd in it).

Note the 3/4 time signature here, which shifts back to the 4/4 groove established earlier in the song by the addition of a fourth beat in measure 5. As long as you count out the quarter note beats in each measure, this type of shift shouldn't prove to be too difficult. You'll need a loose, limber picking hand for all of the six-string strumming in this part, so remember to stay relaxed, and try pivoting at the wrist rather than the elbow. Sawing away with the whole arm is inefficient and impossible to maintain for more than a few minutes. Small, controlled movements are essential.

"What Would You Say" Pre-Chorus Riff from *Under the Table and Dreaming*

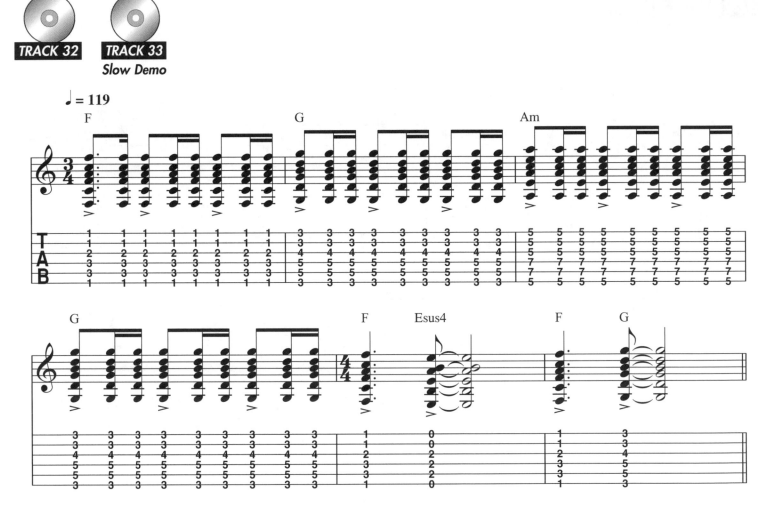

Written by David J. Matthews
© 1994 David J. Matthews (ASCAP)
International Copyright Secured   All Rights Reserved

CHAPTER 6

Single-Note Lines Redux: Increasing the Difficulty Quotient

In this chapter, we'll return to single-note playing and look at a bundle of increasingly challenging phrases while reading notes in a variety of locations on the neck. The goal is to build coordination between the two hands and overall knowledge of the fingerboard.

This first example accompanies Boyd Tinsley's violin solo on "Too Much" and is played entirely on the A and low E strings. Use your index finger for notes on the 2nd fret and middle finger for those on the 3rd and 5th. The short diagonal lines leading to the Es in measures 2, 4, and 6 indicate a slide, which should be performed by placing your pinky on the A string's 5th fret and immediately sliding up to the 7th while pushing down on the string. The 3rd-fret Gs on the low E string in measures 2 and 6 should be played with the index finger.

"Too Much" Violin Solo Riff from *Crash*

TRACK 34

Written by Dave Matthews Band
© 1996 Carter Beauford, Boyd Tinsley, Stefan Lessard, LeRoi Moore, and David J. Matthews (ASCAP)
International Copyright Secured   All Rights Reserved

This next example is from the instrumental section at the end of "Drive In Drive Out." Notice the 6/8 time signature, which indicates six beats per measure, with an eighth note lasting one beat. The fingering is a simple matter here, as your index, middle, and ring fingers should take care of all of the notes on the 1st, 2nd, and 3rd frets, respectively (stay *strictly* in this position). Remember that in the case of the tied notes, play only the 1st note and not the 2nd to which it is tied. In other words, the lines in measures 4 and 6 begin on beat 2, not 1.

"Drive In Drive Out" Outro Riff from *Crash*

Written by David J. Matthews
© 1996 David J. Matthews (ASCAP)
International Copyright Secured   All Rights Reserved

Let's jump back to the beginning of the same song and look at the opening phrase. The line moves mainly between the open A, D, and G strings, with the ring finger taking care of the 4th-fret F♯ and C♯ notes. The only note on the low E string, G, should be played with the middle finger. Remember that in the 6/8 time signature, a 16th note lasts half a beat, so any combination of two 16ths or a 16th note and a 16th note rest will total a single beat.

"Drive In Drive Out" Intro Riff from *Crash*

The final line from this song begins with the index finger on the low E string's 5th fret. The ring finger is then used to play both the A- and D-string 7th-fret notes, outlining a three-note power chord shape. Don't lift the finger to jump from one string to the next—flatten it into a barre instead. Take note of the octave shape here as well, with the higher A (the 3rd note in the sequence) two frets up and two strings over. While it's useful to know where the octave equivalent of any particular pitch can be found, it's also a shape Matthews employs frequently, as in the low and high Gs in measure 3 (we'll talk more about "shapes" later). During the descending sequence that begins in the 2nd half of measure 1 and continues through measure 2, move to 2nd position, using your pinky on the 5th fret, your ring finger on the 4th, your middle finger on the 3rd, and your index finger for the 2nd-fret notes.

"Drive In Drive Out" Coda Lick from *Crash*

In the following lick from "Captain," you'll need to apply a slight *palm mute* by laying the side of your picking hand lightly across the strings right at the point where they meet the bridge. Experiment with right-hand placements to find one that's comfortable for you; the further forward (toward the neck) you are, the less you'll hear in terms of specific pitches, making the line more of a rhythmic, percussive part and less of a melodic one. Use your pinky for each of the 6th-fret, D-string notes, with your middle finger on the A string's 4th fret and your ring and index fingers on the low E string's 5th and 2nd frets, respectively. The stretch in measure 3 may be further than you're used to, but keep reaching for it and your hand will gradually "learn" to open up and make these kinds of leaps possible.

"Captain" Bridge Riff from *Busted Stuff*

The next lick, also from "Captain," employs a repeated rhythm with a quarter note falling on the fourth beat of each measure. While not terribly demanding from a technical standpoint, it takes you up the neck to 8th and 9th position for the first time.

"Captain" Outro Riff from *Busted Stuff*

The lick below is played by violin and saxophone, and interjects occasionally as a kind of instrumental response to Matthews' voice during "So Much to Say." It's played in 12th position and is based on the moveable A minor pentatonic scale discussed earlier. The first note, played on the "and" of beat 1 should be taken by the ring finger on the G string's 14th fret. Stay strictly in this position and your other fingers will fall into line to finish out the phrase in measure 2.

"So Much to Say" Horn/Violin Fill from *Crash*

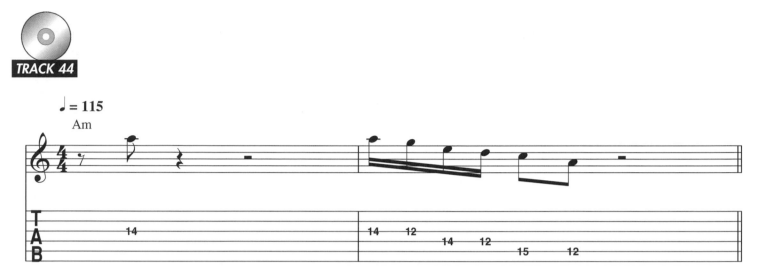

Now let's look at three licks from "Louisiana Bayou," a song propelled by a wide variety of single-note, overdubbed guitar parts. The biggest challenge here will likely be the recognition of the numerous "broken" 16th note rhythms in the lines. Be sure to count out each phrase, using your 16th note verbalizations ("1–ee–and–a, 2–ee–and–a," etc.). Don't just listen to the recording or "feel" it out: You should know, with certainty, where each and every note falls in the measure *and* in each individual beat.

The first lick, played in 4th position, also introduces two vital new techniques: the *pull-off* and the *hammer-on*. These are both indicated by the curved lines beneath the notes on beats 2 and 4 of the example. Don't mistake these symbols for ties, which connect two of the same pitch—a curved line from a higher to a lower pitch indicates a pull-off, while a curved line connecting a lower pitch to a higher one indicates a hammer-on. So what exactly are they?

In each case, we're talking about a method of sounding a second pitch without striking a string with the pick. The pull-off here should be executed by picking the E on beat 2, and then lifting your pinky off the string while simultaneously pulling downwards (just slightly) to sound the D below without re-picking. Obviously, your middle finger will need to be in place on the lower note ahead of time so that the D will be heard clearly. In the case of the beat-4 hammer-on, play the C♯ with your index finger, and then "hammer" down your middle finger onto the A string's 5th fret to sound the next pitch without re-picking.

"Louisiana Bayou" Single-Note Layer #1 from *Stand Up*

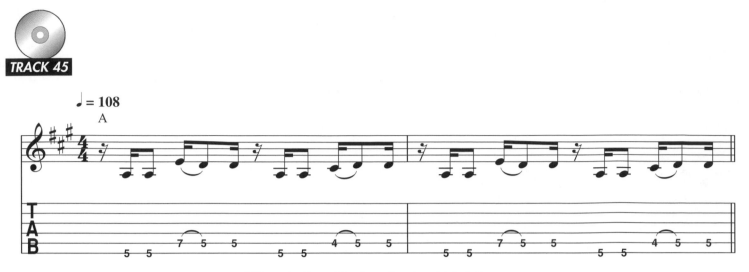

Hammer-ons and pull-offs are used extensively by all guitarists in all styles, often to lend a sense of vocal smoothness *(legato)* to a phrase that would be lacking if every single note were to be picked. These techniques take some getting used to, and will require two new kinds of finger strength: the ability to pull off and down with enough force to sound a lower pitch, and the ability to hammer down with enough force to sound a higher pitch on a fret above.

The next, highly syncopated phrase is to be played in 7th position and includes a hammer-on from the index to the ring finger on beat 2. Don't be shy: Bring that finger down with precision and power. This isn't a terribly challenging line, but aside from that beat-2 hammer-on, everything falls "off the beat"—on an "ee" or an "a." Count out this example and play it as many times as you need to until you have each 16th note in its proper place in the measure.

"Louisiana Bayou" Single-Note Layer #2 from *Stand Up*

Here's a bit of a tough one as regards both rhythm and fingering. Let's talk about the latter subject first. Essentially, this is to be played in 14th position, with your index finger on the 14th fret of both the B and G strings. Don't lift the finger as you switch strings, but rather, "roll" it down, flattening it to grab the G-string notes as needed. The phrase begins in 12th position, with your index finger taking the G at the 12th fret of the same string. Reach out and grab the second note (D on the B string's 15th fret) with your *middle* finger, allowing you to shift up into 14th position and play the third note of the phrase (B) with your ring finger. The rhythmic intricacies of the phrase are equally subtle. Each three-note, 16th note grouping begins on the beat and includes notes on both the "ee" and "a" (second and fourth 16th notes, respectively). However, the addition of broken triplets on beat 3 of the first measure and beats 1 and 3 of the second make the overall line much more difficult to "feel." If you recall our earlier discussion of the topic *(A Crash Course in Rhythm)*, eighth note triplets divide a single beat into three equal pieces. What makes this lick particularly challenging is the omission of the first of those pieces as indicated by the eighth note rest that begins each triplet bracket, and the close juxtaposition of beats divided into three and four units (i.e., triplets and straight rhythms, respectively).

Try the following exercises that may help you to get this together. First, tap out slow quarter notes with your foot while tapping a steady stream of triplets on a tabletop with your hand. After a few measures, remove the first tap on each beat to simulate the broken triplet phrasing found in the lick. Next, keep the quarter note pulse going with your foot while you alternate sets of triplets and 16th notes (i.e., groups of three and four notes). Once you can perform both exercises accurately, you'll be ready to take on the lick below.

"Louisiana Bayou" Single-Note Layer #3 from *Stand Up*

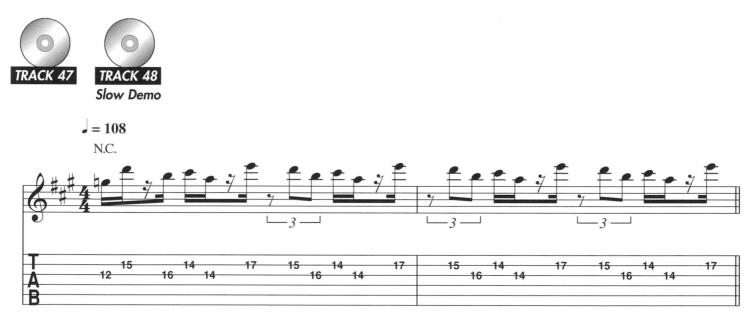

The central riff from "Warehouse," shown below, goes by pretty quickly and requires you to double-pick each note in the phrase. You'll want to slow this one *way* down and really take your time building up to the actual song tempo. Be patient—if you're getting through this by the skin of your teeth, you're working much too fast. This riff employs an "extended" fingering, in which you need to use your index finger on the 7th fret, your middle finger on the 9th fret, and your ring finger and pinky fingers on the 10th and 11th frets, respectively.

"Warehouse" Verse Riff from *Under the Table and Dreaming*

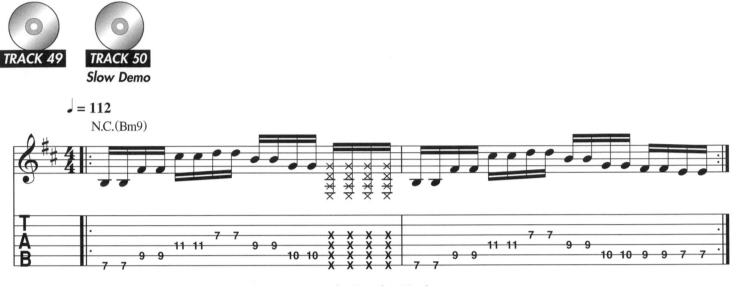

Okay, here's a short, crazy little lick. The rhythm here is a sextuplet on each beat. A *sextuplet* essentially consists of two 16th note triplets in the space of a quarter note, dividing it into six equal pieces. Each beat should be fingered 1–2–3–4–3–2, meaning that you'll have to shift up quickly at the beginnings of beats 2, 3, and 4 to place your index finger on the fret vacated by the middle finger a split second before. This one goes by fast, so take your time getting it up to speed or it'll merely disintegrate into a sloppy mess.

"Too Much" Solo Fill from *Crash*

Finally, the eight-measure excerpt below includes the single-note accompaniment to the first verse of "Too Much." This one is challenging, primarily from a rhythmic standpoint. It's basically a steady stream of 16th notes, most of which should be muted by simply laying your fretting hand lightly across the D string without pushing down. Use your index and middle fingers to play the 2nd- and 4th-fret notes that break up the muted tones throughout. The unpredictability of the placement of these notes can make this a tough little phrase, so break the example up measure by measure, only adding another after you've mastered the previous chunk. Don't miss the various pull-offs in the riff either. By the way, the dots beneath the notes in the final measure indicate that they are to be played *staccato*, or very short in duration.

"Too Much" Verse Riff from *Crash*

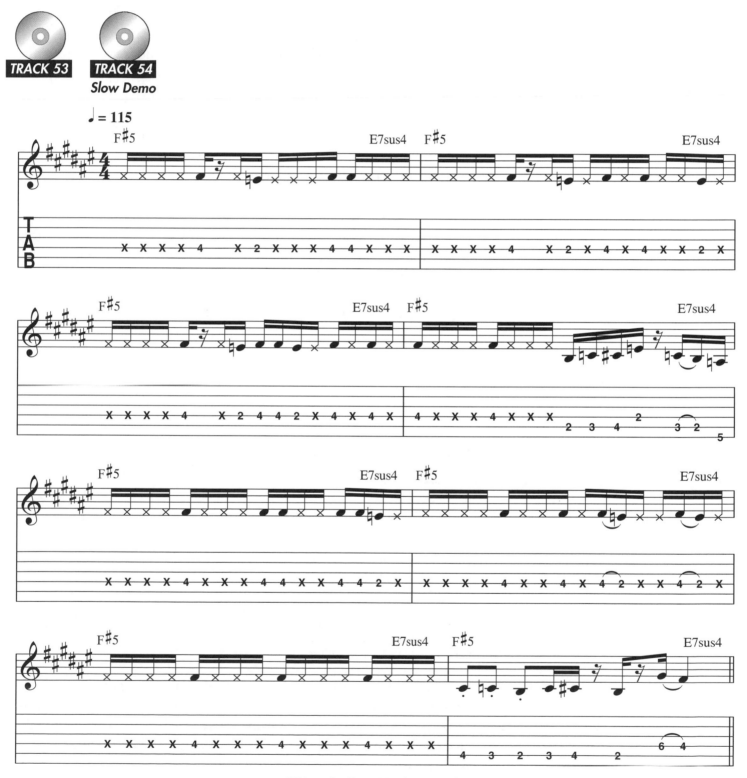

Written by Dave Matthews Band
© 1996 Carter Beauford, Boyd Tinsley, Stefan Lessard, LeRoi Moore, and David J. Matthews (ASCAP)
International Copyright Secured   All Rights Reserved

CHAPTER 7

More on Octaves, Plus a Taste of Dave Matthews' Unique Chord Style

In this chapter, we'll examine Matthews' use of *octaves*—two notes an octave apart, played simultaneously—and take a peek at some of the unusual chord *voicings* (the way the notes in a chord are arranged) unique to his playing style.

Octaves

In the previous chapter, we looked at an example from "Drive In Drive Out" that outlined the octave shape along the lower strings. You can find the higher octave of any single note on the low E or A string merely by going up two frets and two strings. In other words, if you play a 5th-fret A on the low E string, the next, higher A can be found on the D string's 7th fret. However, playing octaves on the higher strings requires a slight adjustment because of the tuning of the B string. If you're on the D or G string, the higher octave iteration of any particular pitch will be up two strings and *three* frets. For instance, the C on the G string's 5th fret is mirrored an octave above on the high E string's *8th* fret. Let's take a look at some examples and all will become clear!

This first lick is from the measure immediately preceding Matthew's vocal entrance on "What Would You Say." Instead of playing both the high and low notes together, you bounce back and forth between G on the low E string (3rd fret) and G on the D string (5th fret). Use your index finger for the lower pitch and your ring finger for the higher pitch. Examine the rhythms in the phrase carefully before taking it to your axe.

"What Would You Say" Intro Fill from *Under the Table and Dreaming*

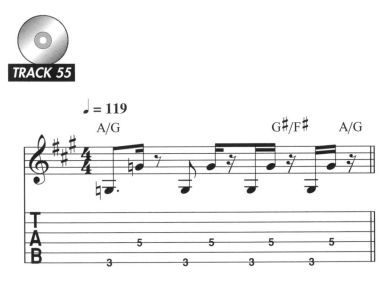

TRACK 55

Written by David J. Matthews
© 1994 David J. Matthews (ASCAP)
International Copyright Secured   All Rights Reserved

Now, let's look at simultaneous octaves played on the higher strings. The next example—a layered part played above the chorus chords in "Where Are You Going"—is merely a D played in octaves over and over again, allowing you to put all of your focus on your fretting hand. Because of the further stretch involved here, you'll want to use your pinky on the high E string's 10th fret. The secret to this lick (and all octave playing) is to flatten the lower-string finger—in this case, the index finger—ever so slightly to prevent the unused, open string between the two pitches from ringing. It's an awkward technique at first, and one that you'll have to be very conscious of performing correctly, but if you work on your octave playing consistently, it's a move that will soon become second-nature.

"Where Are You Going" Chorus Octaves from *Busted Stuff*

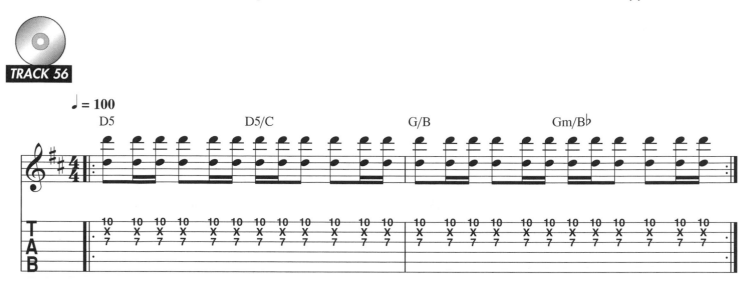

Let's try one more—a trickier phrase from "Drive In Drive Out" that will have you moving the lower-string octave shape around a bit. Begin the riff with your ring finger on the D string's 5th fret and your index finger, flattened slightly to mute the open A string, on the low E string's 3rd fret. At the end of the first measure, keep your fingers pressed down on the strings and *slide* the entire shape up four frets to the B octaves without lifting off. Measure 3 relocates the shape down two frets without sliding, while the fourth measure returns to the song's main single-note theme examined earlier in Chapter 6.

"Drive In Drive Out" Chorus Riff from *Crash*

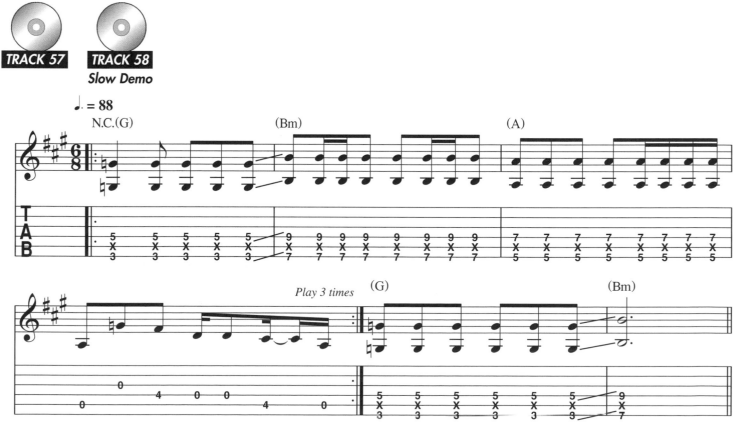

Dave Matthew's Chord Style

A handful of iconoclastic songwriters have created their own harmonic vocabularies by employing unusual chords and chord voicings in their work. Dave Matthews is no exception, with unique sounds that pop up frequently in his songs.

One of these is a ringing open string in the middle of an otherwise normally-fingered chord, higher up along the neck. The well-known intro to "Too Much," excerpted below, is a prime example, as the open D string is heard in the middle of each of the four different chords. The D/F♯ should be played with the index and middle fingers on the low E and G strings, respectively (by the way, "D/F♯" is what's commonly referred to as a *slash chord*—the D is the actual chord, the F♯ is the note that's *in the bass,* or the lowest note of the chord). For both the G and B♭ chords, use the index finger on the low E string and the middle finger on the G string, while the Bm chord calls for the middle and ring fingers on the low and high notes.

"Too Much" Intro Riff from *Crash*

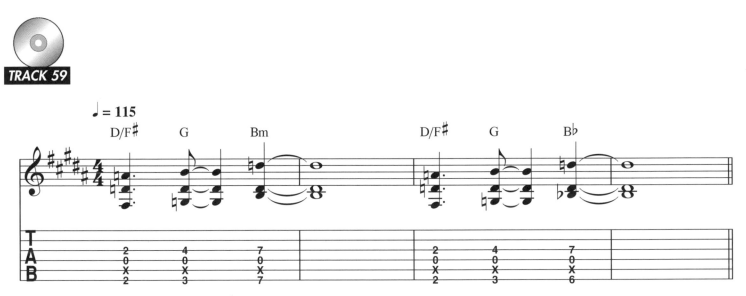

Written by Dave Matthews Band
© 1996 Carter Beauford, Boyd Tinsley, Stefan Lessard, LeRoi Moore, and David J. Matthews (ASCAP)
International Copyright Secured   All Rights Reserved

The 6/8 bridge section of "Rapunzel" excerpted below begins with a D octave shape that also includes a unison—the open D string and the A string's 5th-fret D. The other chords in the phrase (B♭ and Csus2) employ the same, open-string, ringing-in-the-middle arrangement we observed in the previous example. While the entire riff can be played with your ring finger remaining stationary on the G string's 7th fret, you may want to rearrange your fingers to play Csus2. By placing your index finger on the G string, you'll be able to use your middle finger to get to the C on the low E string's 8th fret, an easier task than using the pinky in the same spot. You'll likely find it easier to mute the open A string with this finger as well.

"Rapunzel" Bridge Riff from *Before These Crowded Streets*

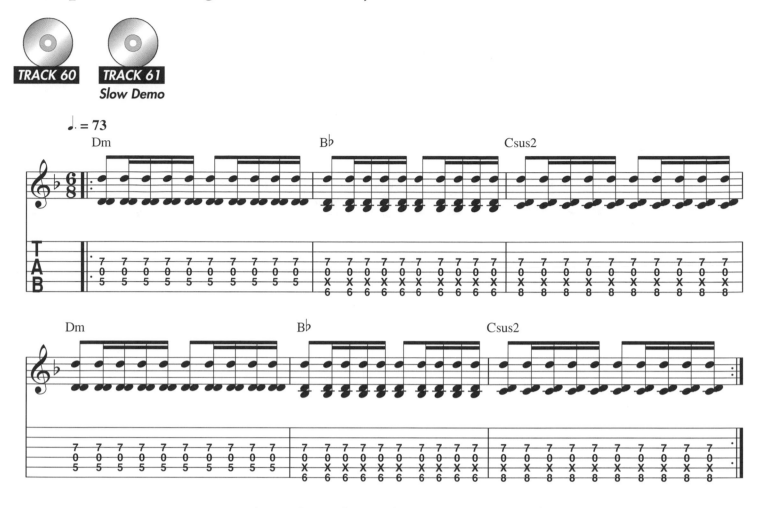

The following example, from "Crush," employs a *drop D tuning* in which the low E string is tuned down a whole step to D. Play the D on your A string's 5th fret, and then tune down your low E string accordingly so the two pitches match (an octave apart).

In the first four measures, use your ring finger to barre the D and G strings at the 4th fret, and then play the same tones with your ring and pinky fingers in the second half of the example, allowing the open B and high E strings to ring above. You'll need to curve your index finger somewhat awkwardly in the final two measures to barre the low E and A strings at the 2nd fret while still allowing the open highest two strings to ring.

"Crush" Outro Riff from *Before These Crowded Streets*

Drop D tuning:
(low to high) D-A-D-G-B-E

♩ = 94

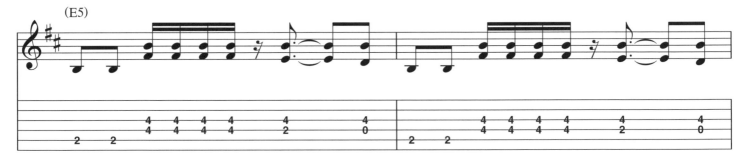

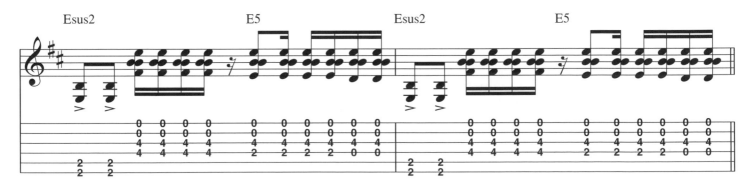

Written by David J. Matthews
© 1998 David J. Matthews (ASCAP)
International Copyright Secured   All Rights Reserved

The next example combines ringing tones on the upper strings with moving pitches below—a favorite Matthews compositional device. Use your ring finger to play the Ds on the B string's 3rd fret throughout the phrase. This one calls for a fair amount of precision: You'll have to pick carefully while you skip from string to string, allowing everything to ring above while you use your index and middle fingers to play the shifting roots on the A and low E strings.

"Where Are You Going" Interlude Riff from *Busted Stuff*

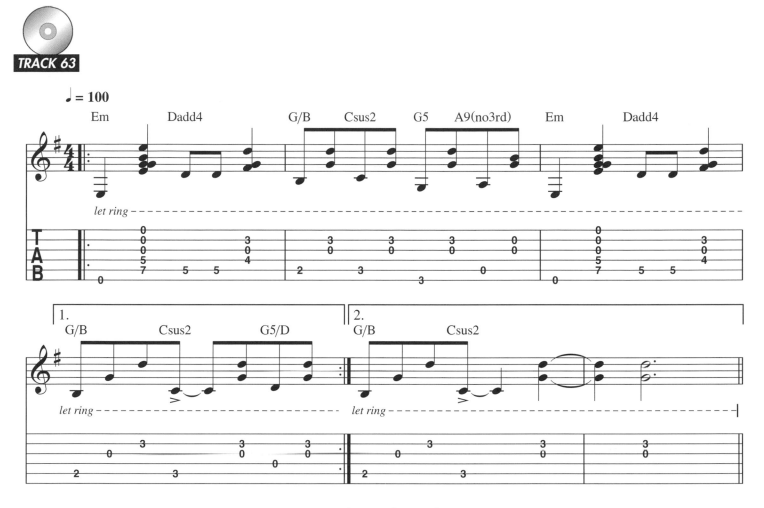

This intricate little riff from "Captain" combines full chords, single notes, and *double stops* (two notes played at once). It also includes a number of difficult voicings that may stretch your fretting hand further than ever before. Don't be discouraged if you can't play them all immediately: The hand *will* open up and make these kinds of leaps if you work slowly and consistently toward them. The C#m(add9) chord should be played with your pinky on the low E string, which will place your middle finger on the A string and your index and ring fingers in a power chord shape on the D and G strings. The G#m, Bm, and A chords all employ the same fingering: ring finger on the low E string (flattened slightly to mute the open A), index finger on the D string, and pinky on the G. Don't overlook the 2/4 measure, or the interesting way in which the first four measures are condensed into a two-measure phrase later in the example.

"Captain" Verse Riff from *Busted Stuff*

Written by David J. Matthews
© 2002 David J. Matthews (ASCAP)
International Copyright Secured   All Rights Reserved

CHAPTER 8

Odd Time Signatures

If you've been working your way through this book methodically, you've encountered 4/4, 2/4, 3/4, and 6/8 time signatures already. In the examples below, we'll add 5/4, 6/4, 3/8, and 7/8 to the mix, all of which are more difficult to navigate and "feel" properly. The rhythmic and metric trickery Dave Matthews Band performs so well was never before in evidence as much as it was on *Before These Crowded Streets*. Each example in this chapter is pulled from that release, including the first phrase, from the interlude that follows the conclusion of "The Dreaming Tree."

The squiggly lines above the Gs in measures 1 and 3 indicate *vibrato*, a slight wavering of pitch created by pushing the string up and down (toward the ceiling and floor) rapidly—but a *very short distance*. Play these notes with the ring finger, allowing you to line up your other fingers behind it and enlist them to aid in the pushing and pulling. Vibrato is often used to mimic the "shaking" effect a vocalist will apply to a sustained pitch. It should be a subtle effect, and one that's used sparingly. Overly wide vibrato can create a wacky, comical effect that's undesirable in pretty much any contemporary playing situation.

The first time signature shift in the example is to 2/4, so we merely lop off the last two beats of a 4/4 measure, and then return to the top. In the second ending, a measure of 3/8 transitions us to a 6/8 groove featuring sliding octaves on the low E and A strings. The changing of the time signature's bottom number (from 4 to 8) constitutes a *metric modulation*—an alteration of not only the number of beats per measure but also of the basic pulse. The eighth note in the previous time signature has become the new "beat," so it's essential to count out the transition. Don't rely on "feel" or guesswork here. Count out the final 4/4 measure in eighth notes. Each of these syllables will represent a single beat in the 3/8 and 6/8 time signatures:

"1–and–2–and–3–and–4–and–1–2–3–1–2–3–4–5–6."

Remember, each of the syllables above should be exactly equal in length. If this seems confusing to you, take your time to examine the music closely, verbalize and tap out the different time signatures and modulations, and count along with the recording in the manner illustrated above. It may take a moment to grasp, but in the end, it isn't any more complex than simple mathematics.

By the way, I mentioned "second ending" a moment ago. The way this works is that you play the first three measures, and then the first ending (under the bracket with the "1"), and then follow that repeat symbol so you play those first three measures again. But on this second pass through, don't play the first ending, play the *second ending* (under the bracket with the "2"), and then continue on with the rest of the music. If this sounds confusing, listen to the recording of this example on the CD—all will be made clear.

"The Dreaming Tree" Interlude from *Before These Crowded Streets*

The opening riff from "Rapunzel" sets up a 5/4 groove that culminates in a measure of repeated C and G/B chords in 6/4. It's not particularly hard from an execution standpoint, but it is deceptively tricky in the way that it obscures the *downbeat* (beat 1) of each measure. As you count out the phrase, use the two eighth notes on beat 2 and quarter note rests on beat 3 of the 5/4 measures to help center yourself. The 6/4 measure includes four "pairs" of C and G/B chords that displace the beat. It's particularly "twisty," so it's imperative that you know exactly where everything falls in the measure. Once again, use the two eighths notes on beat 2 to center yourself. The third G/B chord falls precisely on beat 5 and can serve as another landmark in the madness of this metric wilderness. At the risk of sounding like a broken record here—*COUNT*. There's simply no other way to get a handle on this kind of material.

"Rapunzel" Intro Lick from *Before These Crowded Streets*

This next example, an introductory phrase from "The Dreaming Tree," introduces a few new wrinkles. The 7/8 time signature (seven eighth notes per measure) is equivalent to a measure of 4/4 with its final eighth note lopped off. An eighth note lasts a single beat here, resulting in a two-16th-notes-per-beat scheme, rather than the four we'd find in a measure of 4/4. As you count the phrase out loud, make sure you drop the last syllable from the word "seven" (just say "sev") so that each beat is precisely the same length.

Additionally, the riff calls for a type of *hybrid picking* in which you use the pick (held between the thumb and index finger, as always) to play all of the notes on the G string, while you pluck the high E string notes with your picking hand's ring finger, letting it all ring out for the duration of the phrase. As for your left hand, use your index finger and pinky to play the 2nd- and 4th-fret notes on the G string, respectively. The middle finger will take care of the F♯s on the high E string's 2nd fret—just be sure to hammer down with enough force to sound the pitch as indicated.

"The Dreaming Tree" Intro Riff from *Before These Crowded Streets*

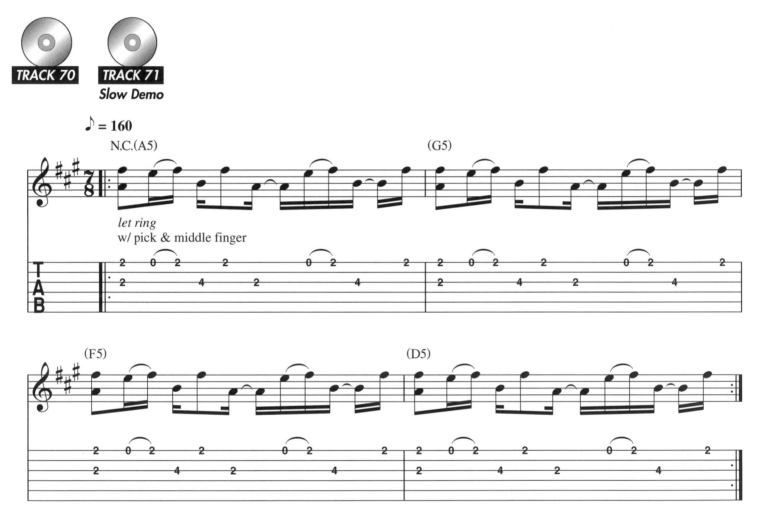

Written by David J. Matthews and Stefan Lessard
© 1998 David J. Matthews and Stefan Lessard (ASCAP)
International Copyright Secured All Rights Reserved

We remain in 7/8 for the following example from the chorus of the same song, employing the same strumming pattern in each measure. This phrase combines three open-position chords (A, G, and D) with an F barre chord. The repetitive nature of the rhythms makes this a fairly easy riff if you're able to transition to each new chord voicing smoothly. As you count your way through it, it may help to divide up each measure into two chunks of four and then three beats. The quarter note at the beginning of the phrase lasts for beats 1 and 2, the eighth note that follows falls on beat 3, and the two 16th notes immediately after begin on beat 4. The final three strums of each measure are syncopated and fall "off the beat," landing in the spaces following beats 5, 6, and 7.

"The Dreaming Tree" Chorus Riff from *Before These Crowded Streets*

TRACK 72

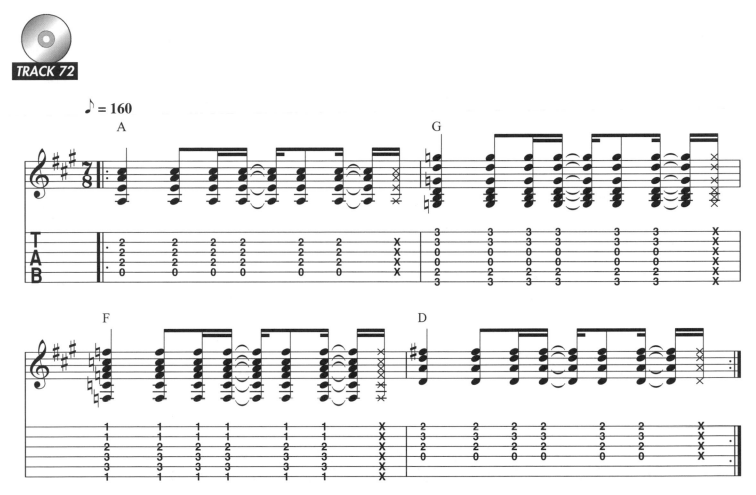

Written by David J. Matthews and Stefan Lessard
© 1998 David J. Matthews and Stefan Lessard (ASCAP)
International Copyright Secured   All Rights Reserved

The 7/8, single-note riff shown below should be played entirely in 2nd position, with your index finger taking all 2nd-fret notes and your middle, ring, and pinky fingers on the 3rd, 4th, and 5th frets, respectively. The sole exception here is on the final two notes of the phrase, which should be played by hammering on from your middle finger to your pinky on the G string. Subtle details really make this excerpt come to life. Carefully observe the various palm-mute markings, staccato dots, hammer-ons and pull-offs encountered throughout.

"The Dreaming Tree" Verse II Riff from *Before These Crowded Streets*

CHAPTER 9

Classic Dave Matthews Band Riffs

We'll, we're getting close to the finish line, and that means that it's time to learn some of the classic guitar parts that make the songs we've been examining so memorable. If you've done your due diligence and worked your way methodically through each of the previous chapters, you'll have built a foundation of solid musicianship and guitar technique on which to construct your own unique playing style. Now let's get to those riffs!

"What Would You Say" was Dave Matthews Band's first big hit, and the riff in the opening measures, shown below, provides the basis of the groove that got it all started. The funky, percussive phrase begins with a middle-finger slide up the low E string from the 3rd to the 5th fret. Slide down the G string with your index finger, and then up the B string with your *pinky*. Matthews' somewhat unorthodox fingering allows you to then grab the A at the end of beat 3 with your middle finger, while your index finger gets to the B on the G string's 4th fret. In measure 2, use your index finger to barre the D, G, and B strings at the 2nd fret and to execute the half step bend-and-release on the B string that follows.

But what is this *bend-and-release?* A *bend* is when you change the pitch of a note (upwards, that is) by pulling or pushing a string with a fretting finger. It takes a while to get this technique down, so we're giving you just a taste of it here. With your index finger, fret and pick the C♯ and then pull the string downwards (without picking it again) until the pitch goes up one half step. Then, release the bend, keeping your finger on the string until you hear that C♯ again; only then should you remove your finger from the string.

"What Would You Say" Verse Riff from *Under the Table and Dreaming*

Now let's take a look at the "jam" section that occurs later in the tune and provides the backing for LeRoi Moore's and guest John Popper's (of Blues Traveler fame) respective saxophone and harmonica solos. This is a typically ornate Dave Matthews rhythm part that combines both full and partial chords, muted tones, double stops, and single notes. Play the A7sus4 chord with your middle, index, ring, and pinky fingers on the A, D, G, and B strings, respectively. Swap the middle and ring fingers to adjust for the A7 chord that follows. There's a pull-off from the 3rd fret to the open low E string in the second measure: Remember to pull toward the floor instead of merely lifting off the fretboard. Matthews ends the phrase with a return to the sliding octave shapes we've encountered in numerous earlier examples.

"What Would You Say" Sax Solo Riff from *Under the Table and Dreaming*

Written by David J. Matthews
© 1994 David J. Matthews (ASCAP)
International Copyright Secured   All Rights Reserved

The riff below opens the band's second major-label release, *Crash*. As the song unfolds, it's clear that while it shares a deep kinship with the band's previous work—and with songs like "What Would You Say," in particular—the group has grown and honed their songwriting and playing with laser-like precision. Dave begins this one with a middle-finger slide up the E string to the 5th fret; he then uses his ring finger to barre the top three strings above. Follow up by sliding to the G string's 6th-fret C♯ with your middle finger, and then quickly drop down to grab the low F with your index finger. Begin measure 2 with a ring-finger slide to the low E string's 10th fret, and once again drop down to grab the low G with your index finger.

The final note in this measure is a *harmonic*, created by laying your pinky gently on the G string above the fret wire (not the wood) and striking the string without pressing down (if this doesn't sound satisfactory, try lifting your fretting finger up from the string simultaneously, or a fraction of a second after you pick it). You should be able to produce a clear, bell-like tone with this method, but like all new techniques, it may require a bit of practice before your harmonics really start to shimmer. Listen to the recording on the accompanying CD to get an idea of what it should sound like.

"So Much to Say" Verse Riff from *Crash*

Written by David J. Matthews, Peter M. Griesar, and Boyd Tinsley
© 1996 Colden Grey, Ltd. (ASCAP)
International Copyright Secured   All Rights Reserved

Let's take a look at a clavinet (a type of electric piano) riff arranged for guitar from the interlude of "Louisiana Bayou." Use your picking-hand fingers (thumb, index, middle, and ring) to grab the strings rather than strumming or picking them each individually. Use your fretting-hand index finger to barre the D, G, and B strings for the A chord, thus allowing you to grab the G on the low E string that follows with your middle finger. The Dm/F chord should be played with your index finger on the low E string's 1st fret and your ring finger and pinky on the G and B strings above. From there, you'll return your index finger to its 2nd-fret barre position and grab the A-string 5th- and 4th-fret notes with your pinky and ring fingers, respectively.

"Louisiana Bayou" Interlude Riff from *Stand Up*

Written by Dave Matthews Band and Mark Batson
© 2005 Colden Grey, Ltd. (ASCAP); and Bat Future Music, administered by Songs of Universal, Inc. (BMI)
International Copyright Secured   All Rights Reserved

The following two excerpts from "Crush" return us to the drop-D tuning we encountered earlier, which requires you to lower the low E string a whole step to D. This first one is a fun, rhythmically propulsive riff that shouldn't tax your technical prowess too much. Simply barre the low E and A strings with your index finger to sound the Gsus2 and Asus2 chords, expanding your barre to add the D string for the E5 chord found later in the phrase.

"Crush" Pre-Chorus Riff from *Before These Crowded Streets*

Drop D tuning:
(low to high) D-A-D-G-B-E

♩ = 94

Written by David J. Matthews
© 1998 David J. Matthews (ASCAP)
International Copyright Secured   All Rights Reserved

Play the Fsus2 chord that begins this riff with your index, middle, and pinky fingers on the A, D, and G strings, respectively. It's a simple matter to shift up to the G5 chord later in the measure, and then drop down to barre the three lowest strings at the 10th fret to play the C5 chord in measure 2. The final two measures feature steady eighth note chugging on C5 and E5 power chords (the latter using the four-note voicing employed in the previous example). Use all downstrokes with the pick in these measures to lend them just the right amounts of heft and percussiveness.

"Crush" Chorus Riff from *Before These Crowded Streets*

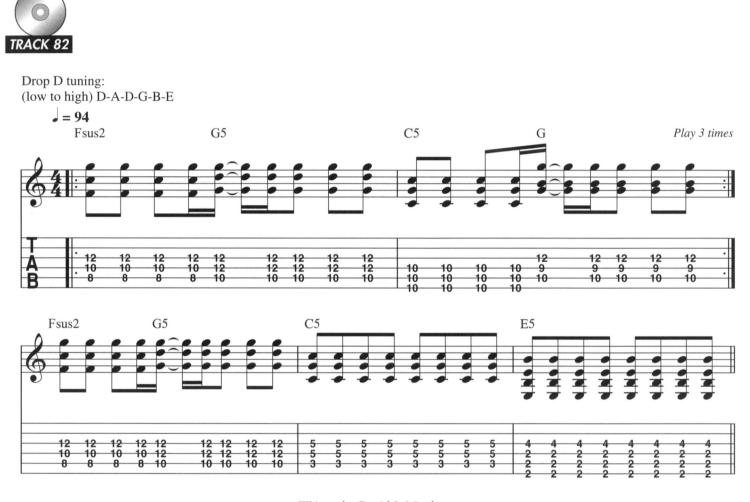

The riff below complements the lower-pitched line from "Rapunzel" examined earlier in our discussion of odd time signatures. You may want to turn back to those pages for a detailed discussion of the 5/4 and 6/4 measures and the rhythmic twists they contain, particularly the repeated shifts from C to G/B in the example's final measure. Regardless, you'll want to have a clear understanding of exactly where each note falls so that you can play this one with confidence. Once that mission is accomplished, take this example to the neck and start with a ring-finger slide up the D string. The Dm7, F, and G shapes should be played with the ring, index, and middle fingers on the D, G, and B strings, respectively. Play the A and C double stop on the G and B strings with your ring and middle fingers, and then use your index finger to barre the double stops at the 12th and 10th frets. The two-note iterations of the C and G/B chords should be played with a ring-finger barre (5th fret of the G and B strings) and, in the case of the latter chord, an index-finger barre to which you will quickly add your middle finger, hammering down onto the G string's 4th fret as indicated in the notation.

"Rapunzel" Intro Riff from *Before These Crowded Streets*

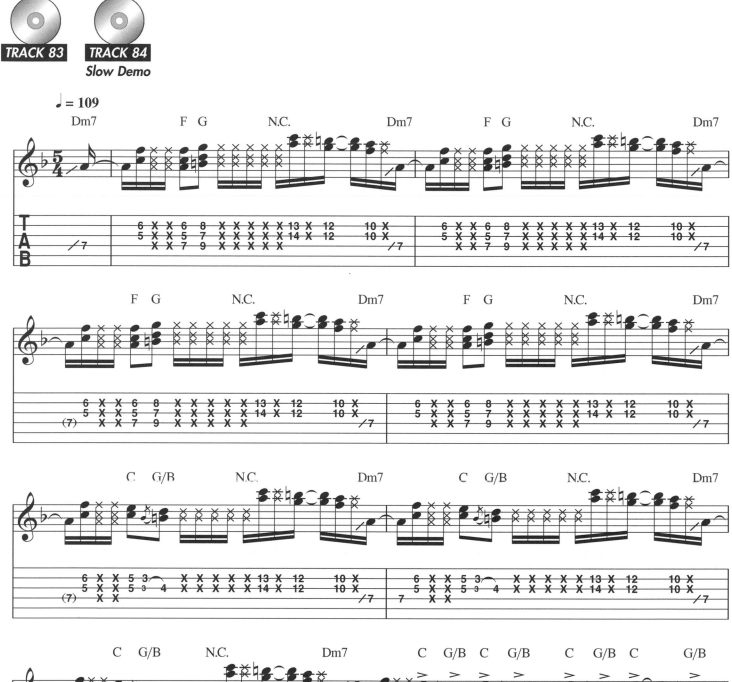

Written by David J. Matthews, Stefan Lessard and Carter Beauford
© 1998 David J. Matthews, Stefan Lessard and Carter Beauford (ASCAP)
International Copyright Secured   All Rights Reserved

Dave Matthews accompanies himself on the "Rapunzel" verses with this choppy little riff made up of octaves, power chords, and double stops. Keep your pinky on the D string's 5th fret throughout the phrase, and stretch your hand to grab the F on the low E string's 1st fret for each F9 chord. By keeping the pinky stationary, you'll be able to shift from C to G/B simply by moving from your middle finger to your index finger on the A string's 3rd and 2nd frets. Once again, I implore you to count out any challenging rhythms here, particularly in the final two measures, which include a metric modulation from 4/4 to 7/8. Remember, not only is the number of beats per measure changing (from four to seven), but the basic pulse is also, so that the eighth note in the first time signature becomes the new pulse in the second. Verbalize it like this:

"1–and–2–and–3–and–4–and–1–2–3–4–5–6–7 ('sev')."

Each of the above syllables should be absolutely equal in length. Note the removal of the final syllable of the word "seven." If we said the entire word, we'd likely give the final syllable a beat of its own, which would make for eight eighth notes and completely defeat the purpose of the exercise. Good luck—this one is tough!

"Rapunzel" Verse Riff from *Before These Crowded Streets*

Written by David J. Matthews, Stefan Lessard and Carter Beauford
© 1998 David J. Matthews, Stefan Lessard and Carter Beauford (ASCAP)
International Copyright Secured   All Rights Reserved

The 4/4 outro jam at the end of "Rapunzel" provides a bit of welcome relief in its relative simplicity, particularly as it comes close on the heels of myriad metric modulations and time signature shifts. The G7 and F7 chords here should be played with the index finger on the low E string, flattened slightly to prevent the open A string from ringing. This one should be a piece of cake after running the gauntlet of rhythmic pain encountered earlier in the song!

"Rapunzel" Outro Riff from *Before These Crowded Streets*

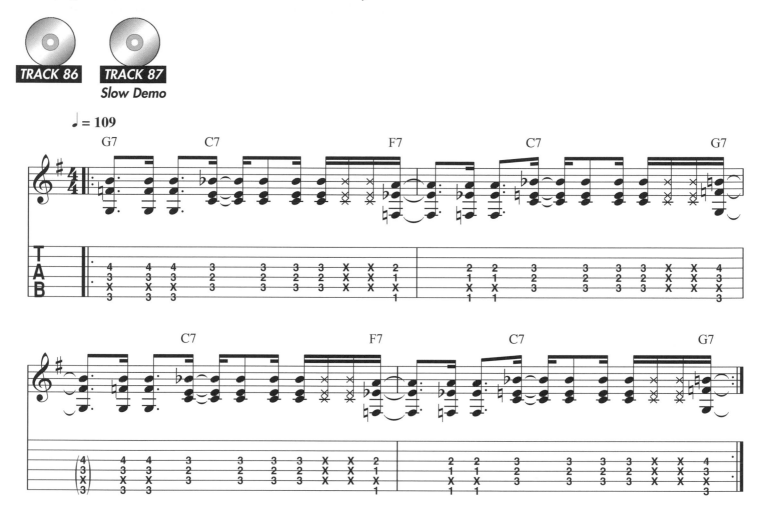

Our final two examples are taken from the immensely popular single "Where Are You Going" and are fun and relatively easy to play (about time, huh?). The first measure below is played four times as an intro with the addition of a layered 12-string guitar. As Matthews' vocal enters, this subtly shifting riff begins. Start things off with a hammer-on from the open G string to the 2nd fret using your index finger. Try leaving your ring finger in place on the B string's 3rd fret throughout the phrase, adding your middle finger to the low E string's 3rd fret in measure 2 and your index and pinky fingers to the A and D strings, respectively, in measure 3. Simply jump the index finger up a string to the D string's 2nd fret in the final measure. Do your best to let all of the strings ring for their natural durations as the phrase unfolds, to create a rich, warmly resonant sound.

"Where Are You Going" Verse Riff from *Busted Stuff*

A final example—the chorus riff from "Where Are You Going"—remains. Leave your ring finger stationary on the B string's 3rd fret throughout the phrase and move the other fingers around accordingly, once again allowing all of the strings to ring out as much as you possibly can.

"Where Are You Going" Chorus Riff from *Busted Stuff*

Written by David J. Matthews
© 2002 David J. Matthews (ASCAP)
International Copyright Secured   All Rights Reserved

If you've resisted the urge to jump around through these pages, and instead have put in the long hours of work to get here by moving carefully from chapter to chapter, you are to be commended. If you haven't, go back and take a look at the things you've skipped. Musical growth, or growth in any aspect of life, requires dedication to attacking the things that are the most difficult, not those that you can already do well. So laugh off the boredom, the confusion, and the repetition of learning something new and challenging. Embrace the torment and become a better musician instead! You'll thank me when it's over and you're flying skillfully across the fretboard.

Know this: Every musician faces technical shortcomings at every stage of their development, from abject beginner to seasoned veteran. The best players refuse to shy away from addressing these shortcomings. There is a close relationship between your tolerance for hard work and the speed with which you'll improve. Every hard hour spent in the practice room will be paid back with a lifetime's worth of pleasure at the joy of making music well. Enjoy!

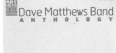

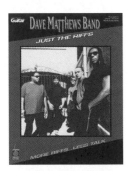
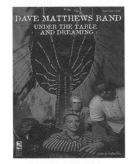
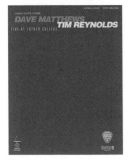